lookbook cookbook

Simple, Delicious, Gluten-Free & Vegan
Dishes for Fashion–Loving Foodies

JESSICA MILAN
founder of the website Lookbook Cookbook

PAGE STREET
PUBLISHING CO.

PAGE STREET
PUBLISHING CO.

First published in 2015 by
Page Street Publishing Co.
27 Congress Street, Suite 103
Salem, MA 01970
www.pagestreetpublishing.com

Distributed by Macmillan; sales in Canada by The Canadian Manda Group; distribution in Canada by The Jaguar Book Group.

18 17 16 15   1 2 3 4 5

ISBN-13: 978-1-62414-121-8
ISBN-10: 1-62414-121-8

Library of Congress Control Number: 2014950272

Cover and book design by Page Street Publishing Co.
Photography by Jessica Milan

Printed and bound in China

Page Street is proud to be a member of 1% for the Planet. Members donate one percent of their sales to one or more of the over 1,500 environmental and sustainability charities across the globe who participate in this program.

DEDICATION

Dedicated to all you fashion-loving foodies

INTRO 7

SMOOTHIES + SHAKES 9

NO-FUSS FOOD 41

HAPPY BRUNCHING 79

APPS + SNACKS 101

SOUPS + SALADS 127

SWEET TREATS 155

TIPS + TRICKS 190

ABOUT THE AUTHOR 191
ACKNOWLEDGMENTS 191
INDEX 192

INTRO

This is *Lookbook Cookbook*, a combination of my healthy vegan recipes with photos of cool girls indulging in them. *LBCB* originally started off as a blog a couple of years ago featuring dessert recipes and all things sweet. Now it's time to bring on the real food!

All of these recipes keep things simple without the use of meat, dairy, gluten or soy. This isn't a crazy diet or a fad, this is just an easy way to have fun in the kitchen while staying healthy to boot. Dairy and meat are not replaced with their vegan substitutes, but instead with the freshest of fresh ingredients.

You don't have to be vegan to enjoy these recipes, but I do hope you like your greens! All kidding aside, there is still plenty of other good stuff to be had in these pages. Fiesta Layer Dip (p 102) or Raspberry Frostie (p 17) perhaps?

I believe that food should be fun, eating should be embraced and calories should never ever be counted. And rarely will you have to count when you are eating so fresh and clean. Unless of course you flipped straight to the dessert chapter, but a little indulgence never hurt anyone in that case. Everything in moderation, right?

I also don't mind at all if you switch up the recipes in this book. Don't like Brussels sprouts or green peppers? You can make easy substitutions when you feel like it, swapping any veggie for another. Just don't skimp on the veg altogether, or don't tell me if you do. Every recipe in this book can also be halved or doubled.

So, enjoy these recipes, always put a little love into your cooking and don't count, just eat! Check out some of the tips and tricks at the end of this book first and then let's get started.

—Jessica

SMOOTHIES + SHAKES

Whether you're an on-the-go or a laze-in-bed type, smoothies are the perfect way to start the morning. You can get an early boost of fresh fruit or veggies and go on happily with your day. For an extra-healthy start, try anything green. For an extra-fun start, Double Fudge Shake (18) anyone?

All of these recipes can be easily doubled if you are two.

ORANGE MANGO LASSI

MAKES 1

Coconut milk and mango just belong together, as shown in this deliciously smooth and creamy concoction.

1 cup (165 g) mango, diced
½ cup (120 mL) freshly squeezed orange juice
½ cup (120 mL) canned, full-fat coconut milk
1 tbsp (12 g) blonde coconut nectar, optional
Ice, optional

Add all ingredients to your blender, except the ice, and mix well. Serve over ice if you want it more chilled, and enjoy right away.

SAHARA >

ACAI BLAST

Thanks to the perfect mix of acai and blueberries, this smoothie tastes too good to actually be good for you, but that's not the case! It's jam-packed full of antioxidants and fruity goodness.

½ cup (120 mL) vegan milk of choice

½ (3½ oz [100 g]) acai smoothie pack

½ cup (75 g) fresh blueberries

1 medium banana

1 tbsp (12 g) blonde coconut nectar

Add all ingredients to your blender and mix well. Enjoy immediately.

< HATTIE

STRACCIATELLA SHAKE

MAKES 1

My favorite ice cream flavor, vegan-ified and smoothie-fied for your sipping pleasure.

1½ cups (205 g) coconut ice cream

½ cup (120 mL) vegan milk

½ of a medium banana

⅛ cup (25 g) organic dark chocolate chips

¼ tsp natural vanilla extract

Add all ingredients to your blender and mix, leaving some chocolate chunks. Drink it up before it melts.

ALICE >

RASPBERRY FROSTIE

MAKES 1

This smoothie is the perfect mixture of tart raspberries and sweet banana. So refreshing!

¾ cup (95 g) fresh raspberries

½ cup (120 mL) purified water

1 medium banana, peel removed and frozen

1 tbsp (12 g) blonde coconut nectar, optional

If you don't have a frozen banana, try frozen raspberries instead. Add all ingredients to your blender and mix well. Enjoy while still cold.

< AUDREY

DOUBLE FUDGE SHAKE

MAKES 1

Double the fudge, double the fun! This decadent treat has a double dose of both with dark chocolate and cacao.

¼ cup (45 g) organic dark chocolate chips

¾ cup (180 mL) vegan milk

1 medium banana

1 tbsp (7 g) cacao powder

Melt the chocolate chips in a small saucepan with a splash of the vegan milk. Use a rubber spatula and stir constantly so it does not burn.

When the chips are melted, add all ingredients to your blender and mix well. Enjoy!

CAILIN >

BERRY BLASTER

MAKES 1

Three simple ingredients and five minutes in the kitchen bring you my favorite way to get an easy blast of berries.

1 cup (140 g) frozen mixed berries

½ cup (120 mL) vegan milk

1 medium banana

Add all ingredients to your blender and mix well. Enjoy!

< NIKKI

TROPI-GREEN SMOOTHIE

MAKES 1

Dream of all things tropical while you sip away on this morning delight, and feel happy knowing you are getting an extra dose of greens while you do.

1 cup (140 g) fresh papaya, diced

1 cup (30 g) packed baby spinach

¾ cup (180 mL) pure coconut water

½ of a medium banana

Add all ingredients to your blender and mix. Add a bit of extra coconut water, if you please. Enjoy immediately.

RAVEN >

BLUE MELON

It doesn't get much easier than this fresh mix of fruit, with no added sweetener or milk.

1 cup (180 g) chopped green melon

½ cup (75 g) blueberries

1 medium banana

¼ cup (60 mL) purified water

Add all ingredients to your blender and mix well. Enjoy!

< JESSICA

ALMOND DATE SMOOTHIE

MAKES 1

Creamy almond butter is sweetened naturally with dates and banana in this amazing delight.

1 cup (240 mL) vegan milk

¼ cup (40 g) dried pitted dates

1 banana

1 tbsp (10 g) smooth almond butter

⅛ tsp natural vanilla extract, optional

Add all ingredients to your blender and mix well.

MINJI >

PEACHES + CREAM

MAKES 1

Fresh peach paired with banana and milk makes for a creamy treat that is sure to please.

½ cup (120 mL) vegan milk

1 large ripe peach, diced

1 medium banana

1–2 tbsp (12–25 g) blonde coconut nectar

Add all ingredients to your blender and mix well. Enjoy immediately.

< REBECCA

THE DETOXER

MAKES 1

All things nice with a little bit of spice. Fresh ginger gives an extra kick to this healthy green smoothie.

2 big red apples, diced

1 cup (30 g) baby spinach

1" (2.5 cm) piece of fresh ginger, peeled and diced

¾ cup (180 mL) purified water

Add all ingredients to your high-speed blender and mix well. Enjoy right away while still fresh and give a little stir if separation occurs.

ADRIANNE >

CITRUS ZINGER

MAKES 1

Put a little zing in your step with this fresh blend of pineapple, orange and grapefruit.

1 cup (165 g) freshly cut pineapple
½ cup (120 mL) freshly squeezed orange juice
¼ cup (60 mL) freshly squeezed grapefruit juice
2 tbsp (25 g) blonde coconut nectar

Add all ingredients to a blender and mix well. Pass through a mesh strainer to remove all of the pulp, using a spoon to push it through. Garnish with fresh orange and pineapple wedges, if you please. Enjoy it while it's fresh.

< NADINE + ALLEGRA

SUNRISE SMOOTHIE

MAKES 1

Start the morning off right with this simple mixture of bananas, orange juice and strawberries.

½ cup (120 mL) freshly squeezed orange juice

½ cup (75 g) fresh strawberries, diced

1 medium banana

1 tbsp (12 g) blonde coconut nectar, optional

Add all ingredients to your blender and mix well.

COCO >

DRINK YOUR GREENS

MAKES 1

With this recipe you'll get five servings of fruit and veg before your day even starts. Now, that's something to feel good about.

2 medium green apples, diced

2 cups (60 g) packed baby spinach

1 cup (240 g) cucumber, diced

¼ cup (60 mL) purified water

Squeeze of fresh lemon juice

3-5 fresh mint leaves, optional

Add all ingredients to a high-speed blender and mix well. Enjoy immediately before separation occurs.

< ALEX

KEY LIME SMOOTHIE

MAKES 1

Zesty lime makes for a refreshing drink in this creamy mix.

½ cup (120 mL) vegan milk

1 medium banana

1-2 tbsp (12-25 g) blonde coconut nectar

2 tbsp (30 mL) fresh lime juice

¼ tsp fresh lime zest

Ice cubes

Add all of the ingredients except the ice cubes to your blender and mix well. Serve over ice and sip away while it's fresh.

NADJA >

NO-FUSS FOOD

No fuss is more fun! And your time in the kitchen should always be fun. Not to mention the easier food is to make, the sooner it is ready for you to eat.

All of these recipes can easily be doubled or halved, though I never choose to make less when I can have leftovers the next day. If you're serving the rice or pasta dishes as the main event, they will make two generous portions.

STUFFED RED PEPPERS

MAKES 4–6 HALVES

Tasting as good as they look, these will be sure to impress. By the way, this filling tastes amazing on its own, too—just reduce the amount of salt you use a little.

½ cup (85 g) dry quinoa

1 cup (240 mL) purified water

2 medium or 3 small red peppers, cut in half lengthwise and stems removed

2 tbsp (30 mL) olive oil, plus more for braising

1 cup (150 g) white onion, finely diced

½ cup (60 g) zucchini, finely diced

½ cup (60 g) green bell pepper, finely diced

½ cup (75 g) cherry tomatoes, halved or quartered

1 cup (25 g) fresh basil, minced

¼ cup (10 g) fresh parsley, mint or oregano, minced

1 tbsp (15 mL) fresh lemon juice

¾ tsp sea salt

Preheat the oven to 350°F (180°C). Begin to cook the quinoa by heating it in a small saucepan with the purified water over high heat. Bring it to a boil, and then reduce heat to low. Cover with a lid and allow to gently simmer for around 10–15 minutes until all of the water is evaporated. When ready, remove from heat, fluff it with a fork and set aside.

While the quinoa is cooking, coat the red peppers in olive oil. Place them on a baking sheet and bake them for 20–25 minutes, depending on how well-done you like them.

While the peppers are cooking, add 1 tablespoon (15 mL) of olive oil and the onion to a frying pan over medium-low heat. Cook for around 5 minutes until the onions are translucent, stirring often. Add the zucchini, mix and cook for an additional 5 minutes. Add the green pepper and cook for another 3 minutes before removing the pan from the heat.

Add the quinoa to the frying pan along with the cherry tomatoes, fresh herbs, 1 tablespoon (15 mL) olive oil, lemon juice and sea salt. Mix thoroughly.

When the red peppers are removed from the oven, generously fill them with the quinoa mixture so that it is almost overflowing. If there's any leftover quinoa, enjoy it on its own. Put the red peppers back in the oven for 10 minutes to cook once more. Serve hot.

ROOKIE >

FAJITAS TOSTADAS

Anything that you can put guacamole and salsa on counts as a winner to me. This recipe is virtually foolproof and can be served in gluten-free soft tortillas or on tostadas. It makes between 6 and 10, depending on how big they are and how full you make them, but definitely be prepared to eat more than one (or two for that matter).

1 or 2 medium white onions

1 medium red bell pepper

1 medium yellow bell pepper

1 medium green bell pepper

1 medium zucchini

1 jalapeño, diced, optional

1–2 tbsp (15–30 mL) olive oil

1 tbsp (15 mL) fresh lime or lemon juice

1 tsp cumin

1 tsp sea salt

Mini corn tostadas or soft-shell tortillas

Chunky Guacamole (p 114)

Salsa Fresca (p 102)

Cut all of the veggies into long, skinny strips of the same size.

Heat the olive oil in a large pan over medium-low heat. Add the onions and cook for 5 minutes until translucent. Add the peppers, zucchini and jalapeño. Mix well. Add the lime or lemon juice, cumin and sea salt and mix once more. Cook for around 15 minutes, or until desired tenderness reached, stirring often so they do not burn.

Serve on the tostadas or tortillas with Chunky Guacamole and Salsa Fresca. Enjoy!

< JENICA

VEGGIE PAD THAI

MAKES 2 LARGE SERVINGS

Though it still contains some fun stuff, this is one pad thai you can feel good about eating. Want an extra healthy kick? Try it with coconut sugar instead of cane sugar and omit the peanuts.

NOODLES

8 oz (225 g) vermicelli rice stick noodles

1 tbsp (15 mL) olive oil

½ cup (75 g) white onion, finely diced

2 garlic cloves, peeled and grated

3 cups (215 g) small broccoli florets, stems removed

3 or 4 green onions, diced

1 cup (160 g) bean sprouts

SAUCE

¼ cup (60 mL) tamari

¼ cup (50 g) organic cane sugar

3 tbsp (45 mL) fresh lime juice

2 tbsp (35 g) tomato paste

GARNISH

½ cup (75 g) unsalted peanuts, crushed

Fresh lime wedges

Green onions, diced

Boil the water for the noodles and cook as the package directs. Be careful not to overcook as they can fall apart easily if you do.

Add the olive oil, white onion and garlic to a large frying pan over medium-low heat. Cook for 5 minutes until the onions turn translucent. Stir often so they do not stick to the pan.

Add the broccoli and green onion and cook for another few minutes until desired tenderness is achieved. Remove from heat until the noodles are done.

Mix the ingredients for the sauce in a small cup and whisk with a fork. Put the peanuts in a small bowl and crush them using the back of a spoon or throw them in your food processor for a few seconds.

Strain the noodles when they are ready, add them to the frying pan and turn it back on to low heat. Throw in the bean sprouts and the sauce. Mix thoroughly and allow it to heat up for a minute or so.

Remove from heat, transfer to bowls and add peanuts, lime wedges and green onion on top.

CHANEL >

QUINOA YAM PATTIES

MAKES 4 SMALL PATTIES

These delicious patties are slightly crunchy on the outside and full of soft sweet potato, warming you with every bite. Try them with your favorite toppings on a bed of lettuce or with a gluten-free bun.

1½ cups (200 g) sweet potato, peeled and diced into ½" (1 cm) cubes

¼ cup (45 g) quinoa

½ cup (120 mL) purified water

1 tbsp (15 mL) olive oil, plus more for frying

¼ cup (40 g) white onion, finely diced

1 garlic clove, minced

½ cup (80 g) cooked chickpeas, drained and rinsed

½ tsp sea salt

½ tsp chili powder

Bring some water to a boil in a small saucepan and add the sweet potatoes to it. Cook for around 15 minutes until they are soft. When they are ready, drain and put them in a small bowl and mash them until all the chunks are gone.

While the potatoes are boiling, cook the quinoa by heating it and the purified water in a small saucepan over high heat. Bring it to a boil, and then reduce heat to low. Cover with a lid and allow to gently simmer for around 10–15 minutes until all of the water is evaporated. When ready, remove from heat, fluff it with a fork and set aside.

Add the olive oil, onion and garlic to a frying pan over medium-low heat. Cook for around 5 minutes until the onion turns translucent. Remove from heat and set aside.

Add the chickpeas to a bowl and use a fork to mash them into a paste. Add the onion, quinoa and mashed potatoes when ready. Throw in the salt and chili powder and mix well. Use the palms of your hands to make 4 even patties.

Add a generous amount of oil to the frying pan and cook each patty. Wait until golden-brown underneath, about 5 minutes, and flip carefully. Cook the other side until golden-brown as well.

< LAURYN

COCONUT CURRY ON RICE

SERVES 2

With creamy coconut and a light curry flavor, this meal is a staple for me. I often keep cooked rice on hand and the sauce takes just minutes to whip up. The less time I have to wait for this one, the better.

RICE

1 cup (210 g) uncooked brown basmati rice

2 cups (475 mL) purified water

SAUCE

1 tbsp (15 mL) olive oil

1 cup (150 g) white onion, finely diced

½ tbsp (7 g) freshly grated ginger

1–1½ tbsp (10–15 g) curry powder

1–2 tbsp (12–25 g) organic cane sugar

1 tsp sea salt

¼ tsp cayenne powder, optional

1 (14 oz [414 mL]) can full-fat coconut milk

1 red pepper, diced

Fresh lime wedges, to garnish

Add the rice and water to a large pot and cook over high heat. When the water begins to simmer, reduce heat to low, give it a quick stir and put a lid on it. Cooking time may vary slightly, but usually it is around 20 minutes. Try not to peek too much until the end to see if it is ready. When it is ready, remove from heat, fluff it with a fork and put it aside for a few minutes.

When the rice is almost finished, add the olive oil, onion and ginger to a frying pan over medium-low heat. Cook for around 5 minutes, or until the onion turns translucent, stirring often. Add the curry, sugar, salt and cayenne. Mix.

Add the coconut milk and heat until it begins to gently simmer. Stir often so it does not stick. Cook for several minutes until sauce reaches desired thickness. Add the red peppers in the last few minutes so they still retain some of their crunchiness. Serve over rice, garnished with fresh lime wedges.

HATTIE >

POLENTA PIZZA

MAKES 2 SMALL PIZZAS

This one satisfies all pizza cravings and leaves you feeling good after. I like to put onion, red pepper and zucchini on mine, but most veggies would work just fine.

CRUST

½ cup (85 g) cornmeal

1½ cups (355 mL) purified water

½ tsp sea salt

1 tbsp (15 mL) olive oil

TOPPINGS

½ tbsp (8 mL) olive oil

1 cup (150 g) diced white onions, red pepper and zucchini

⅓ cup (80 mL) marinara sauce

Line a baking sheet with parchment paper. Cook the cornmeal, water and sea salt in a small pot on medium heat, whisking constantly with a fork. Cook for about 10 minutes until a thick oatmeal consistency is created. Remove from heat, stir in the olive oil and set aside for 1 or 2 minutes to cool. Take spoonfuls of the mixture to make two medium circles on the baking sheet, both about ½-inch (1.2 cm) thick and 5 inches (12.7 cm) wide. Set in the refrigerator for 30 minutes to set.

When ready to cook the crust, preheat the oven to 450°F (235°C). Cook for around 20 minutes until the top of the crust begins to harden and turn golden-brown. In a small frying pan over medium-low heat, add the olive oil and cook the veggies for around 10 minutes.

When the crust is done baking, remove from the oven and add the marinara sauce. Don't add extra as it could make it soggy. Add the veggies on top and put back in the oven for a few minutes. Serve hot.

< MOUNA

TEX-MEX POTATO SKINS

MAKES 4 HALVES

These crispy potato skins are filled with spicy black beans and topped with fresh avocado. Enjoy with a side of Cashew Cream or Salsa Fresca (both recipes are on p. 102).

2 large russet baking potatoes

1 cup (240 g) cooked black beans, drained and rinsed

½ cup (75 g) white onion, finely diced

2 medium tomatoes, diced

1 or 2 jalapeños, minced

1 tbsp (15 mL) olive oil

1 tsp chili powder

½ tsp paprika

½ tsp sea salt, plus a little extra for after the potatoes have cooked

¼ cup (60 mL) olive oil, for braising

1 medium avocado, diced

1 green onion stalk, diced, to garnish

Preheat the oven to 425°F (220°C). Use a fork to poke several holes throughout each potato to allow steam to come out. Put in the oven and bake for around 45 minutes, or until you can cut through it with a knife and the center is cooked.

While the potatoes are baking, make the filling so it can marinate. Add the black beans, onion, tomatoes, jalapeño, 1 tablespoon (15 mL) olive oil, chili powder, paprika and ½ teaspoon sea salt to a bowl and mix well. Add the juices from the tomatoes as well.

When the potatoes are ready, remove them from the oven and allow them to chill for several minutes. Once they are cool enough to handle, cut each one in half lengthwise and carefully use a knife and spoon to scoop out the center, leaving a thin layer of potato around the skin. If you accidentally take out the potato right down to the skin, just mash a little bit back in.

Generously coat all sides of the potato skins with ¼ cup (60 mL) olive oil and a sprinkle of sea salt. Evenly fill each one with the filling. Put back in the oven and bake for around 15 minutes, or until the skin is crispy on the outside. Remove from the oven and garnish with the avocado and green onions.

MINJI >

SWEET CHILI SOBA

SERVES 2

Anything with coconut milk just really gets me. These noodles are light and fresh, with a creamy sauce and crisp bell peppers. I like to go light on the spice, but if you like it hot, go big with the chili pepper and flakes.

NOODLES

8 oz (230 g) gluten-free soba noodles

2 cups (300 g) mixture of yellow, red and green pepper, cut into thin 2" (5 cm) strips

1 or 2 medium green onion stalks, cut into 2" (5 cm) strips

SAUCE

½ cup (120 mL) full-fat coconut milk

¼ cup (45 g) tahini

1 quarter–1 whole fresh red chili pepper, minced (for extra spice, use the whole pepper)

2 tbsp (30 mL) fresh lime juice

2 tbsp (30 mL) tamari

1 tbsp (12 g) blonde coconut nectar

½ tbsp (7 g) fresh ginger, diced

GARNISH

Fresh lime wedges

Chili flakes

Extra green onion, cut in 2" (5 cm) strips

Sea salt, to taste

Begin to boil water and cook the soba noodles as directed on the package. To make the sauce, add all of the ingredients to your blender and mix well. Use part of the chili pepper, or all of it, depending on how spicy it is and your preference.

Drain the noodles when they are ready and put back into the pot, followed by the peppers, onion and sauce. Mix well.

Serve in bowls and garnish with fresh lime wedges, chili flakes, extra green onion and a sprinkle of sea salt, if you please.

< ANNA

PASTA PRIMAVERA

SERVES 2

This light and fresh pasta is full of zesty lemon and springtime vegetables that will leave you feeling satisfied. It also tastes great chilled.

PASTA

2–2¼ cups (230-260 g) gluten-free pasta

1 tbsp (15 mL) olive oil

6 garlic cloves, peeled and left whole

2 cups (300 g) cherry tomatoes

1 cup (240 g) asparagus, cut into 2" (5 cm) diagonal strips

1 cup (200 g) snow peas, stems removed and cut in half

1 cup (40 g) packed fresh basil, chopped

SAUCE

¼ cup (60 mL) olive oil

¼ cup (60 mL) fresh lemon juice

1 tsp fresh lemon zest

1 tsp sea salt

Begin to cook the pasta according to its instructions on the package. Add the olive oil and garlic to a large frying pan over medium-low heat. Cook for a few minutes until it becomes fragrant.

Use a fork to poke holes in the cherry tomatoes so they do not burst when cooked. Throw them in the frying pan with the garlic and cook for a few minutes. Stir often so they do not burn. Add the asparagus and snow peas and cook for only a few minutes so they still have quite a bit of crunch left in them. Remove from heat and set aside when ready. Discard the garlic. You can also save a clove or two and grate it into the veggies if you choose.

Mix the sauce ingredients in a small bowl or cup. When the pasta is ready, drain it and remember to rinse it before putting it back in the pot. Add the veggies, followed by basil and the sauce. Mix once more and there you go! Enjoy hot or chilled.

ANNA >

SWEET POTATO CHILI

MAKES 4 BOWLS

With hearty red beans, sweet potato and chili powder, this one will be sure to warm you up. Garnish with nachos for some extra fun.

1 tbsp (15 mL) olive oil

1 medium or large sweet potato, peeled and cut into ½" (1 cm) cubes

2 cups (300 g) red onion, finely diced

1 garlic clove, minced

1 tbsp (10 g) chili powder

2 tsp (10 g) sea salt

1 tsp cumin

A pinch of cayenne pepper

4 medium tomatoes, diced

1½ cups (265 g) cooked red kidney beans, drained and rinsed

2 cups (475 mL) purified water

Add the olive oil to a large pot over medium-low heat. Add the sweet potato, onions and garlic. Mix to coat in the oil. Cook for around 5 minutes before adding the chili powder, salt, cumin and cayenne. Give another quick mix and add the tomatoes and beans.

Allow to cook for around 10 minutes, until liquids begin to form at the bottom of the pan. Add the water, increase heat and bring to a boil. Once it begins to boil, give it a stir, turn the heat down to low and allow to gently simmer for around 45 minutes or until desired thickness is reached. This will thicken up a little bit after it has cooled.

< BECKY

BLACK BEAN BURRITO

MAKES ENOUGH FILLING FOR 2 BIG BURRITOS

This burrito is full of raw veggies that will leave you feeling healthy, not heavy. Be sure to use a generous amount of avocado, or switch it up with some guacamole instead. If you are only making one burrito, the beans can last a few days in a sealed container in the refrigerator.

FILLING

2 tbsp (30 mL) olive oil

½ cup (75 g) white onion, finely chopped

1½ cups (300 g) black beans, drained and rinsed

1 tbsp (15 mL) apple cider vinegar

1 tsp cumin

½ tsp sea salt

A few pinches of paprika

BURRITO

1 or 2 gluten-free tortillas

1 medium or large avocado, mashed in a bowl

Tomato, finely diced

Cucumber, finely diced

Jalapeño, diced, optional

A large handful of mixed greens

Sea salt, to season

Add 1 tablespoon (15 mL) of olive oil to a frying pan over medium-low heat. Add the onion and sauté for approximately 5 minutes, or until it turns translucent.

Add the beans to a medium-size bowl and mash with a fork. Add the apple cider, 1 tablespoon (15 mL) of olive oil, cumin, sea salt and paprika directly to the beans and mix well. Add the beans to the onions, mix and heat thoroughly for a few minutes.

Heat each tortilla in a large frying pan over low heat or in the oven on low heat for 1–2 minutes. When heated, lay them out on plates and add desired amount of black beans in a strip down the middle. Be sure to leave space at the tops and sides for folding.

Add the avocado, tomato, cucumber, jalapeño and mixed greens on top of the beans. Be sure to not overfill so the burrito closes well. Sprinkle with sea salt.

Fold the bottom part of the tortilla up over the contents of the burrito so it can contain the food while you eat it. Hold it tightly in place while folding the left side of the tortilla over the filling. Once it is folded over, keep the end of it in place where it meets the food and continue rolling the burrito to close it. Enjoy!

MONTY >

ROASTED RATATOUILLE

SERVES 2—4

Get your daily dose of veg hassle-free with this warming plate. Non-eggplant-lovers, don't be put off. I am one of you and love this one. You can eat it on its own, or serve over rice or quinoa. This also makes for amazing leftovers.

2 cups (300 g) cherry tomatoes

1 medium zucchini

1 medium red pepper

1 small eggplant

1 medium white onion

3 garlic cloves, peeled and left whole

½ cup (120 mL) olive oil

1 tsp sea salt

½ cup (20 g) fresh basil

Preheat the oven to 450°F (230°C). Poke holes in the tomatoes with a fork. Cut the rest of the veggies in uniform 2-inch (5 cm) pieces.

Line a rimmed baking sheet with parchment paper. Place the veggies and garlic on top, coat with the olive oil and salt, and give a mix. Don't spread them too thin or they will burn. You want them to be quite close together to get juicy while they roast.

Cook for 30–45 minutes, checking every 10 minutes or so to give them a stir and make sure they are all cooking evenly. Check more often as you near the end of cooking. They are ready once a nice liquid has formed and they have all softened, without going mushy. Remove from oven when ready and stir in the basil.

< QUINN

SUN-DRIED TOMATO PASTA PESTO

SERVES 2

I'm a sucker for anything with fresh basil—and even more so if that basil is on pasta. And if sun-dried tomatoes are involved as well? Then it's really on. Make sure you use sun-dried tomatoes packed in oil for this one, they make for a better sauce.

PASTA

2–2¼ cups (230–260 g) uncooked gluten-free pasta

1 cup (150 g) cherry tomatoes, halved

Basil leaves, for garnish

PESTO

¼ cup (30 g) raw unsalted sunflower seeds

2 cups (80 g) packed fresh basil

⅓ cup (80 mL) olive oil

½ cup (30 g) sun-dried tomatoes

1 tsp sea salt

Cook the pasta according to its directions. To make the pesto, add the sunflower seeds to your food processor and blend them into a coarse powder. Add the basil, olive oil, sun-dried tomatoes and sea salt. Blend until a paste forms, occasionally stopping to scrape down the sides of the processor with a rubber spatula. Set aside until the pasta is ready.

When the pasta is done cooking, drain it and be sure to rinse it before putting it back in the pot. Throw in the cherry tomatoes, and add desired amount of pesto. I like to use all of it because I like it extra saucy. Garnish with basil leaves and enjoy!

GURINA >

TAHINI RICE BOWL

This dish is full of dark greens, coated in a flavorful sauce and topped with toasted seeds for extra crunch. If you are saving some for later, don't throw in the sauce and seeds until you plan on eating it.

RICE

¾ cup (160 g) uncooked basmati rice

1½ cups (355 ml) purified water

1 tbsp (15 mL) extra-virgin olive oil

1 cup (150 g) white onion, diced small

½ tbsp (3 g) fresh ginger, grated

¼ cup (30 g) mixture of unsalted sunflower and sesame seeds

1 cup (70 g) small broccoli florets, stems removed

1 green onion stalk, chopped

2 cups (60 g) packed baby spinach

SAUCE

¼ cup (60 g) tahini

¼ cup (60 mL) extra-virgin olive oil

1½ tbsp (25 mL) tamari

1 tbsp (15 mL) toasted sesame oil

1 tbsp (15 mL) apple cider vinegar

1 tbsp (15 mL) purified water, optional

Add the rice and water to a medium pot over high heat. When the water begins to simmer, reduce heat to low, give it a stir and put a lid on it. Cooking time can vary slightly, but usually it takes around 20 minutes. Try not to peek to see if it's ready too much until the end. When it is ready, remove from heat, fluff it with a fork and put it aside for a few minutes.

When the rice is almost finished, add the olive oil, white onion and ginger to a large frying pan over medium-low heat. Cook for 5 minutes until the onion turns translucent. Stir often so it doesn't stick to the pan.

Add all the sauce ingredients together in a bowl and whisk well with a fork.

Add the seeds to a small frying pan over medium-high heat. Keep a close eye on them so they do not burn, and stir frequently. After about 5 minutes, they will begin to either brown, become fragrant or pop. Cook for a few minutes more, remove from heat and set aside.

Add the broccoli and green onion to the frying pan with the white onion. Cook them for only a few minutes, so they're still a bit crunchy. Add the rice and spinach and mix once more.

Remove from heat and mix in the sauce, reserving some for garnish. Transfer to two large bowls and cover with a generous amount of toasted seeds and additional sauce as desired.

< CLAIRE

SPEEDY CHEEZY PASTA

SERVES 2

Easy peasy deliciously fake cheezy! This dish takes minutes to whip up and uses nutritional yeast to bring the flavor and fun.

PASTA

2–2¼ cups (230–260 g) gluten-free pasta

1 tbsp (15 mL) olive oil

½ cup (75 g) white onion, diced small

½ cup (60 g) zucchini, diced small

½ cup (60 g) red bell pepper, diced small

1 medium tomato, diced small

SAUCE

1 cup (240 mL) marinara sauce of choice

½ cup (75 g) nutritional yeast

2 tbsp (30 mL) olive oil, optional

½–1 tsp sea salt

Boil the water for the pasta and cook as directed on the package. Heat a frying pan over medium-low heat and add the olive oil, onion and zucchini. Cook for around 5 minutes, stirring on occasion. Add the red pepper and cook for another few minutes before removing from heat and setting aside. To make the sauce, add all of the ingredients in a cup and whisk with a fork.

When the pasta is ready, drain and rinse it well before returning it to the pot. Throw in the cooked veggies, the tomatoes and sauce and mix well. Serve hot.

SERENA >

VEGGIE FRIED RICE

SERVES 2

This meal is almost instant gratification if you keep leftover rice in your fridge, which you will probably want to start doing when you see how easy this is to whip up. Just a quick fry up of some simple ingredients gets you something warm, filling and full of flavor.

RICE

3 cups (585 g) cooked brown basmati rice, left in the fridge for 5 hours or overnight

2 cups (175 g) shredded Brussels sprouts or savoy cabbage

1 tbsp (15 mL) olive oil

2 cups (300 g) white onion, finely diced

½ tbsp (3 g) freshly grated ginger

1 medium red pepper, julienned

4 or 5 green onion stalks, sliced lengthwise and in 2" (5 cm) strips

¼ cup (35 g) sesame seeds

SAUCE

2 or 3 tbsp (30–45 mL) wheat-free tamari

2 tbsp (30 mL) olive oil

2 tbsp (30 mL) toasted sesame oil

1 tbsp (15 mL) apple cider vinegar

Cook the rice ahead of time and let it sit in the fridge to separate for at least 5 hours, but preferably overnight. 1 cup (185 g) dry rice yields 3 cups (585 g) cooked. Refer to page 50 for how to make the rice.

The Brussels sprouts or cabbage can be shredded by thinly slicing it with a sharp knife.

Add olive oil, onions and ginger to a large frying pan over medium-low heat. Cook for around 5 minutes until the onions turn translucent. Stir often so they do not stick.

Add the cabbage or Brussels sprouts, red pepper and green onion to the pan and mix. Cook for another 5 minutes until they begin to soften.

Meanwhile, lightly toast the sesame seeds in another small pan, stirring often so they do not burn. When they begin to darken and become fragrant, about 5 minutes, remove from heat and set aside. Mix the sauce ingredients in a small bowl or cup.

Add the rice and sauce to the veggies and mix well. Stir in most of the sesame seeds, saving some for garnish. Heat everything thoroughly and enjoy!

< ELYSE

CALIFORNIA WRAP

MAKES 1

A few minutes and a handful of basic ingredients gets you this easy and satisfying wrap.

1 large gluten-free rice or corn tortilla

A generous amount of Hummus (p 110)

Baby spinach, a handful

1 avocado, cut into wedges

Tomato slices

Cucumber slices

1 green onion stalk, diced

Sprouts, a handful, optional

Add all ingredients as desired to the center of the wrap, leaving room at the tops and sides to fold. Fold the bottom part of the tortilla up over the contents so it can contain the food while eating it. Hold it tightly in place while folding the left side of the tortilla over the filling. Once it is folded over, keep the end of it in place where it meets the food and continue rolling the wrap from left to right. Enjoy.

ALICE >

ZESTY QUINOA BOWL

SERVES 2

Full of crunch and zest, this quinoa bowl tastes best chilled. Hello, easy leftovers!

QUINOA

1 cup (170 g) quinoa

2 cups (475 mL) purified water

oil, for frying

1-2 cups (180-360 g) sweet potato, peeled and diced into ½" (1 cm) cubes

1 tbsp (10 g) sesame seeds

1 medium green bell pepper, finely diced

¼ cup (40 g) red onion, finely diced

SAUCE

¼ cup (60 mL) olive oil

2 tbsp (30 mL) freshly squeezed lime juice

2 tbsp (30 mL) tamari

2 tbsp (25 g) organic cane sugar or blonde coconut nectar

1 jalapeño, minced

1 tbsp (10 g) fresh ginger, minced

Begin to cook the quinoa by heating it in a small pot over high heat with the water. Bring it to a boil, and then reduce heat to low. Give it a quick stir, cover with a lid and allow to gently simmer for around 10-15 minutes until all of the water is evaporated. Try not to peek too often. When ready, remove from heat, fluff it with a fork and set aside.

After you start the quinoa, coat a small frying pan generously with oil and cook the sweet potatoes over medium heat for 20 minutes or until they are ready. Stir constantly so they cook evenly. They should be soft on the inside and just slightly crispy on the outside.

In another small pan, toast the sesame seeds over medium heat, turning often so they do not burn, about 5 minutes. Mix the ingredients for the sauce in your blender until all the jalapeño chunks are gone.

When the quinoa is ready, throw in the sweet potato, seeds, green pepper, onion and dressing. Mix well. Chill in the fridge for at least 3 hours to let marinate.

< SARAH

HAPPY BRUNCHING

Waking up is easy when you know you have something to eat waiting for you. Whether it's a light and easy fruit salad, or pancakes with extra maple syrup that gets you out of bed, just know that you are covered here. Pair it with a smoothie and you are really off to a great start.

MORNIN' OATS

This breakfast staple is prepped the night before, making it the perfect go-to for the lazy gal's morning. Switch it up by adding your favorite fruit or toasted shredded coconut.

¾ cup (60 g) wheat-free rolled oats

¾ cup (180 mL) vegan milk

2 tbsp (15 g) crushed pecans

½ tbsp (8 mL) pure maple syrup

½ tsp cinnamon

Mix the oats and milk in a glass or bowl the night before you want to eat them. Cover them and refrigerate. The next morning, remove from the fridge and heat in a small saucepan for a few minutes. Add more milk as you please.

Transfer to a bowl and mix in the pecans, maple syrup and cinnamon. And that's it! Enjoy!

ZOE >

VEGGIE QUESADILLAS

MAKES 2

If this doesn't get you out of bed in the morning, then you need to add more avocado to it. Try it with an extra side of guacamole.

1 avocado, diced

1 medium tomato, diced

¼ cup (40 g) white onion, finely diced

1 jalapeño, minced, optional

Fresh lime juice

Sea salt, to taste

Olive oil, just enough for the pan

2 medium corn tortillas

Cashew Cream (p 102) or Chunky Guacamole (p 114), optional side

Put the avocado, tomato, onion and jalapeño in a small bowl followed by a squeeze of lime juice and sprinkle of sea salt. Mix with a fork and mash the avocado a little bit into the tomatoes.

Add a small swig of olive oil to a frying pan over medium-low heat. Add one tortilla and cook it for a minute or so. Add half of the avocado mixture to one half of the tortilla, and fold the other side on top, using the back of the spatula to press down on it. Be careful not to use too much filling, leave a little bit of room at the edges so it doesn't fall out.

Cook for about 2 minutes, until golden-brown on the bottom, before carefully flipping and cooking the other side. Remove from heat when ready, and allow to cool for a few moments. Repeat with the second tortilla. Then use a fork and a sharp knife on a cutting board to cut the quesadillas into quarters or thirds. Put some of the filling back in if it falls out. Enjoy with a side of Cashew Cream or Chunky Guacamole.

< BIANCA + DANI

ZUCCHINI FRITTERS

MAKES 6

These little guys are great on their own or as a side to your main brunching. I like mine with ketchup—extra of course.

1 cup (180 g) grated zucchini

1 cup (225 g) grated potato

1 or 2 medium green onion stalks

2 tbsp (20 g) all purpose gluten-free or rice flour

½ tsp sea salt

½ tsp baking soda

Handful of fresh herbs of choice, minced (I like basil, oregano and parsley)

1 tbsp (15 mL) olive oil

Put the grated zucchini and potato in a bowl and use a clean hand towel or paper towel to absorb all of the water. The more you can get out, the better these will fry up. Put back in the bowl and add the green onion, flour, salt, baking soda and fresh herbs. Mix well.

Add the olive oil to a frying pan over medium-low heat. Place ¼ cup (70 g) spoonfuls of batter onto the pan and gently flatten a little with the back of your spatula. Allow to cook for a few minutes until they become a dark, golden-brown. Make sure the temperature isn't too hot. It's better to cook them slower so the inside cooks evenly. Flip it over when ready and cook the other side as well.

Serve hot as is, or with sauce of your choice.

NIKKI >

STRAWBERRY CREAM PANCAKES

Strawberries and coconut make the perfect pair in this delicious treat, with a generous serving of maple syrup of course.

1½ cups (180 g) gluten-free pancake mix

½ cup (40 g) shredded coconut

¼ cup (50 g) organic cane sugar

1 cup (240 mL) vegan milk

1 tsp pure vanilla extract

1 tbsp (15 mL) coconut or grapeseed oil, plus extra for frying

2 cups (335 g) chopped strawberries, plus more for topping

Coconut Whipped Cream (p 188) and maple syrup, for topping

Add the pancake mix, shredded coconut and cane sugar to a large bowl and mix well. Stir in half of the vegan milk, and the vanilla and oil. Mix once more and add more milk as needed. Stir in the strawberries.

Heat a frying pan over medium heat. Add a drizzle of oil to the pan and add spoonfuls of batter. Flip the pancakes when slightly bubbled on one side and golden-brown underneath, after about 2 minutes. Cook the other side until golden-brown as well.

Enjoy these pancakes warm with Coconut Whipped Cream, maple syrup and fresh strawberries.

< COCO

BERRY PARFAIT

SERVES 1

There's not much to making this morning treat and it's sure to put a smile on your face with its good looks. I prefer to keep it light and simple, but you can also throw in a handful of wheat-free granola, if you please.

1 cup (265 g) sweetened coconut yogurt

Fresh lemon juice and zest

1 cup (150 g) mixed berries of choice

Fresh mint to garnish, optional

If you are using any larger berries like strawberries, dice them into bite-size pieces. Put the coconut yogurt in a bowl and mix in some lemon juice and zest as desired. Pour half of the yogurt into a glass, followed by half of the fruit. Alternate once more with the remaining yogurt and fruit. Garnish with mint and that's it!

ALICE >

BANANA ACAI BOWL

MAKES 1 BOWL

Delicious acai and banana are blended together and topped with your favorite fresh fruit in this easy breakfast bowl.

1 (3.5 oz [100 g]) frozen acai smoothie pack

1 medium banana

1 cup (140 g) frozen mixed berries

¼ cup (60 mL) vegan milk

½–1 cup (85–170 g) fresh fruit of choice, diced

Wheat-free granola, garnish (optional)

Add the acai, banana, frozen berries and milk to your blender and mix until thick and smooth. Use a rubber spatula to scrape down the sides. Transfer to a bowl and top with the fresh fruit of your choice and granola, if you please.

< ANNA

FULLY LOADED PANCAKES

MAKES 6 LARGE PANCAKES

Filled only with things that are fun, these babies are easy to make and aim to please.

1½ cups (180 g) gluten-free pancake mix

¼ cup (45 g) organic dark chocolate chips

¼ cup (30 g) crushed pecans

1 tsp cinnamon

1 cup (240 mL) vegan milk

½ tsp natural vanilla extract

1 tbsp (15 mL) coconut or grapeseed oil, plus more for frying

½ cup (90 g) banana, finely diced

Almond butter and pure maple syrup, for topping

Add pancake mix, chocolate chips, pecans and cinnamon to a bowl and mix well. Stir in half of the milk, and the vanilla and oil. Mix again, adding more milk as needed. Stir in the bananas after.

Add a drizzle of oil to frying pan over medium heat. Add large spoonfuls of batter and flip after about 2 minutes, when slightly bubbled on one side, and golden-brown underneath. Cook the other side until golden-brown as well.

Serve hot with a dollop of almond butter and a drizzle of maple syrup.

BECKY >

CHICKPEA "OMELETTE"

MAKES 1

Who needs the real deal when you can make this hearty version? I fill it with red pepper and green onion, though any veggie can be substituted as long as it's diced small.

½ cup (50 g) chickpea flour

½ tsp sea salt

½ cup (120 mL) purified water

¼ cup (40 g) red bell pepper, finely diced

1 green onion stalk, finely diced

Oil, for frying

1 small avocado, cut into wedges

Slices of tomato

A handful of baby spinach

Add the chickpea flour, sea salt and water to a bowl and whisk well with a fork. Make sure the pepper and onion are finely diced. Add to the batter and mix once more.

Coat a small frying pan with oil and heat over medium-low heat. Add the chickpea batter to the center, and quickly pick up the pan and swirl it around so the batter forms a circular shape. Depending on the size of your frying pan, the batter should ideally reach the edges.

Cook for several minutes, keeping a close eye on it so it does not burn. The top side of the batter should bubble throughout and the sides should begin to turn golden-brown. Take a peek to double check, and then carefully flip it over. Cook the other side for a few minutes before transferring to a plate.

Serve with the avocado, tomato, spinach and whatever else you please. Enjoy!

< JORDAN

BLUEBERRY LEMON JONNYCAKES

MAKES 10 SMALL PANCAKES

Crunchy cornmeal brings a fun twist on everyone's favorite morning cake. Be sure to slather on maple syrup to get the full effect.

1¼ cups (300 mL) purified water

1½ cups (255 g) cornmeal

2 tbsp (25 g) organic cane sugar

1 tbsp (15 mL) grapeseed or coconut oil, plus more for frying

1 tbsp (15 mL) fresh lemon juice

1 tsp natural vanilla extract

½ tsp lemon zest

½ tsp sea salt

¼ cup (60 mL) vegan milk

½ cup (75 g) fresh blueberries, plus more for topping

Maple syrup, for topping

Bring the water to a boil in a small saucepan. Once it begins to simmer, remove from heat, stir in the cornmeal and put a lid on for several minutes.

After 5–7 minutes, remove the lid from the pan and stir in the sugar, oil, lemon juice, vanilla, lemon zest and sea salt. Add part of the milk, making sure it isn't too watery before adding the whole amount. More milk will create thinner pancakes; less milk will create thicker ones. These pancakes should be on the thick side. Gently stir in the blueberries.

Heat a generous amount of oil in a large frying pan over medium-low heat. When the pan is heated, add spoonfuls of batter to it. Cook for around 5 minutes, or until the other side is golden-brown. Be patient because they will crumble if they are not ready. After you flip, gently use the back of your spatula to flatten it slightly. Cook the other side for 4–5 minutes as well. Add more oil to the pan after each round.

Serve hot with maple syrup and extra blueberries, if you please.

CATE >

FRUIT SALAD

SERVES 1

Fruit salad is an easy, healthy dish you can put together in a snap. Take whatever fruit you have from the fridge, chop it up, mix it up, garnish and enjoy.

2 cups (500 g) diced fresh fruit of choice

A squeeze of fresh lime juice

A few pieces of fresh mint

Blonde coconut nectar, optional

Add the fruit to a bowl, with the lime juice, a few pieces of fresh mint and a drizzle of blonde coconut nectar, if you please. Mix well and enjoy!

< CLAIRE

APPS
+ SNACKS

I can easily favor eating several snacks as my main meal. And when the snacks are loaded with all things healthy, I don't feel bad at all about that decision. Chunky Guacamole, Veggie Kebabs and Summer Rolls sound pretty well rounded to me!

FIESTA LAYER DIP

MAKES 1 BIG BOWL

With seven layers of Mexican fun paired with nachos, what a fiesta you will have eating this! The recipe makes a jumbo serving, but I suspect that will not be an issue.

SPICY BLACK BEANS

1 cup (240 g) cooked black beans, drained and rinsed

2 tbsp (20 g) white onion, diced

½ tsp cumin

¼ tsp sea salt

SALSA FRESCA

2 medium tomatoes, finely diced

About ⅓ cup (50 g) finely diced white onion

½ jalapeño, minced

¼ tsp sea salt, plus more to taste

Squeeze of fresh lime juice

CASHEW CREAM

1½ cups (200 g) raw, unsalted cashews

2 tbsp (30 mL) fresh lemon juice

¾ cup (180 mL) purified water

½ tsp sea salt

GUACAMOLE

2 medium avocados, or 3 small

2 tbsp (30 mL) fresh lime or lemon juice

2 tbsp (20 g) white or green onion, minced

1 tsp sea salt

1–2 cups (75–145 g) shredded iceberg lettuce

Diced tomatoes, for garnish

1 or 2 medium green onion stalks, diced

Fresh lime or lemon juice

1 big bag of nacho chips

Blend all ingredients for Spicy Black Beans in your food processor until smooth. Set aside.

In a separate bowl, add all of the ingredients for the Salsa Fresca, including the juices from the tomatoes and mash a little with a fork. This tastes amazing left to marinate for a bit. Set aside.

Make the Cashew Cream by blending the cashews in your food processor into a coarse powder. Add the lemon juice and mix again. Use a rubber spatula to scrape down the sides of your processor on occasion. Add the water and salt and blend into a smooth, creamy liquid. This will keep in the refrigerator for a few days. Set aside.

To make the Guacamole, scoop out the avocado flesh, put it in a small bowl and mash it with a fork, adding half of the lime juice to make it easier to mix. Keep it as chunky or as smooth as you please. Add half of the salt and onions, and taste test to see how much more of each ingredient to use. If you are saving it for later, just be sure to add fresh lemon or lime juice to the top and keep it sealed and refrigerated.

Next, add a layer of the Spicy Black Beans to a clear glass bowl or small casserole dish. Put a layer of lettuce on next. Drain the juices from the Salsa Fresca and add that on top of the lettuce so it catches any excess tomato juice, followed by the Cashew Cream and Guacamole. Garnish with some tomatoes and green onion and dig in! If you aren't eating it immediately, put a generous amount of fresh lime or lemon juice on top of the Guacamole so it doesn't turn brown. Store in the refrigerator.

NATALIE + TONYA >

VEGGIE KEBABS

MAKES 3 OR 4 SKEWERS

It's amazing how basic veggies can give such delicious results after a little bit of marinating and time in the oven. Sometimes it's the simple things!

1 medium white onion

1 medium red bell pepper

1 medium yellow bell pepper

1 zucchini

Oil for greasing

VINAIGRETTE

2 tbsp (30 mL) olive oil

2 tbsp (30 mL) fresh lemon juice

1 tbsp (15 mL) apple cider vinegar

1 garlic clove, grated

½ tsp sea salt

Handful of fresh herbs, minced (I like basil, oregano and parsley)

Submerge skewers in water before you are ready to use them, for at least 20 minutes. This will prevent them from burning in the oven.

Dice all the veggies into 2-inch (5 cm) chunks and put in a medium bowl. Put the vinaigrette ingredients in a small bowl or cup and whisk with a fork. Pour the vinaigrette over the veggies and mix. Allow the veggies to marinate for 20 minutes or up to an hour or two, giving them a stir every once in awhile.

Preheat the oven to 350°F (200°C) when you are almost done marinating the veggies. Poke the veggies onto the skewers, alternating each kind. Place on a lightly greased baking sheet in the oven for 10–15 minutes, or longer if desired. Flip them over once halfway through.

< JULIA

CAPRESE BITES

These tasty little bites are balanced with juicy tomatoes and fresh basil leaves, and look extra cute for your eating pleasure.

1 cup (140 g) raw unsalted cashews

2 tbsp (30 mL) fresh lemon juice

1 cup (25 g) fresh basil, chopped

¾ tsp sea salt

12-15 large, fresh basil leaves

2 cups (300 g) cherry tomatoes

Begin by blending the cashews in your food processor into a coarse powder. Add the lemon juice and blend until as smooth as possible. Use a rubber spatula to scrape down the sides of the processor on occasion. Add the basil and sea salt and blend again until there are no large basil chunks left. Remove from the processor and roll into 12 small balls in the palm of your hand. Transfer to the refrigerator to set for a few hours.

When ready, remove from the refrigerator. Put one cherry tomato on a skewer. Wrap a piece of fresh basil around each caprese and gently place it on each stick after the tomato. Put another tomato on after to sandwich the caprese between. Depending on the size of your skewer, you may want to put another layer of caprese and tomato, or just leave it at that. Store in the fridge until ready to serve.

ROOKIE >

SUMMER ROLLS

MAKES 6—8 ROLLS

This snack is such a fun way to eat raw veggies; it feels way more treat-like than it actually is.

ROLLS

1 medium red bell pepper

1 medium carrot

½ medium cucumber

1 medium or large avocado

2 or 3 green onion stalks

Lemon, if needed

6–8 rice paper sheets, plus extra just in case

1 cup (25 g) fresh basil

Sea salt, to taste

DIP

2 tbsp (25 g) almond butter

1 tbsp (15 mL) tamari

1 tbsp (15 mL) coconut nectar

1 tbsp (15 mL) fresh lime juice

1 tsp fresh ginger, grated

Chili flakes, a pinch or two

Cut the red pepper, carrot and cucumber into skinny 3-inch (7.5 cm) pieces. Cut the avocado into skinny wedges and the green onions in half lengthwise and into 3-inch (7.5 cm) strips. If you aren't eating immediately, squirt some fresh lemon juice on the avocado wedges so they do not brown.

Add some water to a large enough pot to lay the rice sheets down flat in. Heat the water to a temperature that is hot, but not too hot to touch. Have a plate ready to lay the rice paper out on. Place each sheet one at a time into the warm water for around 30 seconds, or until it completely softens. Carefully pull it out of the water and place it down on the plate as flat as you can. These can rip easily, and you might need a few tries to get it right.

Place a few pieces of each veggie and the basil into the center of the rice paper, followed by a pinch of salt. Roll the left and right sides over top of the veggies as tight as you can without ripping it. Fold the bottom part over it, and continue rolling it until it's closed.

To make the dip, mix the ingredients in a small bowl and use a fork to whisk it. Add a small spoonful of water if you feel it needs it. Serve with the rolls.

< HAILS

HUMMUS

MAKES 1 BOWL

Why bother with the store-bought stuff when you can make your own? Whipping the tahini first is the secret to getting this hummus just as creamy and delicious as the real deal. This lasts for a few days in the fridge in a sealed container, as long as you don't eat it all by then.

¼ cup (60 g) tahini

2 tbsp (30 mL) lemon juice

1 tbsp (15 mL) purified water

1 garlic clove

1 tsp sea salt

2 tbsp (30 mL) olive oil

1½ cups (230 g) canned chickpeas, drained and rinsed

1–2 extra tbsp (15-30 mL) of water, as needed

Put the tahini, lemon juice and 1 tablespoon (15 mL) of water in your food processor and mix until thick and creamy. You may need to scrape down the sides of your processor with a rubber spatula.

Add the garlic, sea salt and olive oil and mix once more. Add the chickpeas and blend again until smooth and creamy, once again scraping down the sides with a spatula. Add 1 or 2 more tablespoons (15–30 mL) of water as needed. Store sealed in the refrigerator for a few days, and add extra water again later if it dries up a little.

HONOR >

PERFECT POPCORN

This perfect popcorn is as easy to make as it is fun to eat. The batches I make only come in one size, extra large of course. But use whatever size pot you please and make sure the whole bottom of it is coated in oil.

Olive or grapeseed oil

Popcorn kernels

Nutritional yeast

Sea salt

Generously coat the bottom of a medium-size pot with oil. Don't be shy. Pour in the popcorn kernels as desired, making sure they aren't more than one layer thick. Add more oil if they aren't all coated.

Put a lid on top and put the heat on medium-high. After a few minutes, the oil should begin to sizzle and the popping will begin. Keep a very close eye on the popcorn so it does not burn. Don't take off the lid until it's finished. When the popping noises slow down to around two seconds between each pop, remove from heat. Wait a moment before taking off the lid in case any extra kernels pop.

Put into a bowl and generously season with nutritional yeast and sea salt. Generous is the key word here, as a lot of the salt falls to the bottom. I just save the leftovers for my next bowl because I know I will always be having more than one!

< CLAUDIA

CHUNKY GUACAMOLE

Guacamole makes everything better, so much so that I needed to include this second version with a fun twist.

2 medium tomatoes, diced

½ medium cucumber, diced

½ medium red pepper, diced

2 or 3 green onion stalks

1 small jalapeño pepper, minced

1½ tbsp (25 mL) fresh lime juice

½ tsp sea salt, plus more to taste

2 medium avocados

Add the tomatoes, cucumber, red pepper, green onion and jalapeño to a medium-size bowl. Stir in the lime juice and salt.

Add one avocado to a small bowl and mash it with a fork. When the chunks are removed, stir it into the veggies and mix well.

Remove the flesh of the other avocado with a spoon and dice it into small cubes. Mix the second avocado into the guacamole, leaving the chunks intact. Add more salt, lime or green onion as desired, and serve.

CRISTAL >

JALAPEÑO POPPERS

MAKES 10–12 HALVES

These spicy little guys are stuffed with a creamy filling and baked to perfection. Put a pinch of chili flakes on top if you can handle the extra heat.

JALAPEÑOS

5 or 6 jalapeños

Oil, for braising

Chili flakes, for garnish

FILLING

¾ cup (100 g) raw unsalted cashews

2 tbsp (25 g) nutritional yeast

1 tbsp (15 mL) apple cider vinegar

½ tsp sea salt

2 tbsp (30 mL) purified water

Preheat the oven to 400°F (200°C). Cut each jalapeño in half lengthwise and remove the stems and seeds. Wash your hands after dealing with the seeds. Lightly coat each jalapeño with oil and set aside.

To make the filling, put the cashews in your food processor and grind into a coarse powder. Add the rest of the ingredients and blend into a smooth paste. Remove from the blender and put a generous amount of filling into the hollow of each jalapeño. Put in the oven and bake for around 15 minutes, until slightly crispy and golden on top. Serve hot and garnish with a sprinkle of chili flakes.

< KATHARINE

SWEET POTATO COINS

SERVES 2

You really don't have to do much to sweet potatoes to make them delicious. Here they are baked with sea salt and oil, but you can add some paprika or chili powder, if you please. I also like to have them with guacamole or hummus on the side or sometimes with both.

1 or 2 long, skinny sweet potatoes

Olive oil

Sea salt

Preheat the oven to 400°F (200°C). Line a baking sheet with parchment paper. Wash and scrub the sweet potatoes, leaving the skin on.

Cut the potatoes into ¼-inch (5 mm-) thick circles. Put them on the parchment paper and drizzle some olive oil and sea salt on top. Mix them thoroughly to ensure that they are all coated. Spread them apart on the sheet, making sure they aren't overlapping each other.

Put in the oven and bake for around 35–45 minutes, flipping every 10 minutes or so. Keep a close eye on them toward the end to make sure they do not burn. When they begin to caramelize and get a little crispy around the edges, they are ready.

LINDSEY >

CUCUMBER CUPS

MAKES ABOUT 12

Full of raw veggies and healthy hummus, not only do these look good, but they will leave you feeling good too.

1 medium English cucumber

Sea salt

½ cup (125 g) Hummus (page 110)

¼ small red bell pepper, chopped into 1" (2.5 cm) chunks

6 cherry tomatoes, cut in half

Cut the cucumber into ½-inch (1 cm) round chunks. Carefully use a knife to carve the center out, leaving a layer of the bottom intact. Sprinkle with sea salt and generously fill each center with a dollop of hummus. Stick a piece of red pepper in each one followed by a cherry tomato half. And that's it, enjoy!

< STEPHANIE

VEGGIE TEMPURA

MAKES 2 CUPS (360 G)

Veggies get a little crispy boost with this light tempura batter.

⅓ cup (40 g) gluten-free all-purpose flour mix

⅛ tsp baking soda

½ tsp sea salt

½ cup (120 mL) sparkling water

Olive oil, for frying

½ cup (75 g) red bell pepper, diced into 2" (5 cm) pieces

½ cup (65 g) zucchini, diced into coins

5-6 asparagus stalks, stems removed

Tamari, to serve

Add the flour, baking soda and sea salt to a mixing bowl and sift with a fork. Stir in half of the sparkling water and mix. The amount of water you need depends on the brand of flour you use. Add enough until the batter is liquidy with clumps in it. Mix it, leaving some of the clumps intact.

Heat a generous amount of olive oil in a frying pan over medium heat. Dip each piece of veggie in the batter ensuring that it is fully covered. Put in the frying pan and fry for a few minutes on each side, until they turn golden-brown and crispy. Add more oil to the pan between batches to make sure they fry evenly. Enjoy immediately while hot and serve with tamari on the side.

CHRISTINA >

ZUCCHINI BRUSCHETTA

MAKES 4–6 PIECES

Straight up veggies win again with this healthy spin on an old classic. Make sure to use as large of a zucchini as possible so there is more room to stuff it full of tomato goodness.

1 large zucchini, cut in half lengthwise

1 tbsp (15 mL) olive oil, plus extra for braising

1 large tomato

¼ cup (40 g) white onion, diced

Handful of fresh basil

½ tsp sea salt

Preheat the oven to 350°F (180°C).

Cut the zucchini halves into thirds or quarters, depending on the size of it. Carefully use a knife to remove the center of each piece, leaving approximately ½ inch (1 cm) of it intact, including the skin. Coat it with olive oil and place on a baking sheet.

Finely dice the tomato, onion and basil and mix in a small bowl with the sea salt and 1 tablespoon (15 mL) of olive oil. Fill the center of the zucchinis with as much of the mixture as you can, as it will shrink when roasted.

Cook in the oven for around 15–18 minutes, depending on how well-done you like your zucchini. Remove from the oven when ready and allow to cool for a few moments before enjoying.

< JENICA

SOUPS + SALADS

Soups and salads are my favorites. Such simple and fresh ingredients can give you something so healthy and easy to prepare. And more importantly, they leave room for extra snacks later.

I like my salads big. These ones can all make one jumbo serving, or fill two normal bowls. If you are making it ahead of time, throw the dressing and seeds on at the last minute. And all of these soups taste great as leftovers. Just reheat and add a little bit of water if they have thickened at all.

TAHINI GREENS

MAKES 1 BIG BOWL

This is by far my favorite salad. With a creamy tahini dressing and plenty of toasted seeds, it makes for such an easy way to enjoy your greens.

DRESSING

¼ cup (60 g) tahini

2 tbsp (30 mL) olive oil

1½ tbsp (25 mL) tamari

½ tbsp apple (8 mL) cider vinegar

1 tsp organic cane sugar

Dash of toasted sesame oil, optional

1–2 tbsp (15–30 mL) purified water

SALAD

1 cup (20 g) kale or Swiss chard, stems removed and ripped into bite-size pieces

1 cup (340 g) green cabbage, sliced thin

2 cups (100 g) romaine lettuce

GARNISH

¼ cup (30 g) mixture of raw unsalted pumpkin seeds, sunflower seeds and sesame seeds

Alfalfa sprouts, optional

To make the dressing, add all of the ingredients except the water to a glass and whisk well with a fork. Depending on the thickness of your tahini, you may need to add ½ tablespoon (8 mL) of water at a time to get desired consistency. Dressing should be thick and creamy.

Add the kale or Swiss chard and green cabbage to a large bowl. Pour ⅓ of the dressing on top and mix well so the greens can marinate. Set aside for a few minutes.

Add the seeds to a small frying pan over medium-high heat. Keep a close eye on them and give a shake often so they cook evenly. When they begin to turn brown and pop, after about 2 minutes, leave for a few moments more before removing from heat. Set aside to cool.

Add the lettuce to the salad bowl and mix well. Add a little more dressing as desired, saving some for garnish. Throw some alfalfa sprouts on top and generously add the seeds, followed by another drizzle of salad dressing. Use rubber spatula to get every last drop of it.

ELYSE >

MOROCCAN SOUP

MAKES 4 BOWLS

Spiced chickpeas are the stars of this comforting soup. This tastes great blended smooth, or left with some small chunks in it.

1 tbsp (15 mL) olive oil

2 cups (300 g) white onion, diced small

2 tsp (10 g) sea salt

2 tsp (10 g) cane sugar

1 tsp cumin

1 tsp paprika

Pinch cayenne pepper

3 large or 4 medium tomatoes, diced

4½ cups (685 g) canned chickpeas, drained and rinsed

3 cups (710 mL) purified water

Add the olive oil and the onions to a pot over medium-low heat. Cook for 5 minutes, or until the onion becomes translucent, giving a stir on occasion.

Add the sea salt, sugar, cumin, paprika and cayenne, followed by the tomatoes and chickpeas. Stir once more and then add the water. Increase heat to bring to a boil, then reduce heat and allow to gently simmer for 30 minutes. Give it a stir every 5 minutes or so.

When ready, remove from heat and allow to cool for a few minutes. Completely submerge a hand blender to purée, or allow to cool completely and put it in a normal blender. Serve hot.

< CHRISTINA

CAULIFLOWER "COUSCOUS"

SERVES 1—2

It's not how it sounds! But finely ground cauliflower is comparable to couscous, and gives crunch and texture to this easy salad. Don't skimp on any of these ingredients, they all bring their own unique flavor to otherwise straight-up veggies.

3 cups (225 g) chopped cauliflower, stems removed

1 medium tomato, diced small

½ cup (70 g) cucumber, diced small

½ cup (70 g) black olives, coarsely chopped

¼ cup (40 g) red onion, finely chopped

¼ cup (10 g) fresh basil, minced

¼ cup (10 g) mixture of fresh herbs, minced (I like parsley, mint and oregano)

2 tbsp (30 mL) fresh lemon juice

2 tbsp (30 mL) olive oil

½ tsp sea salt

¼ tsp fresh lemon zest

Make sure the cauliflower stems are completely removed. Add cauliflower to your food processor and pulse into a fine grain. If there are some chunks left, remove the part that is already ground to make it easier to get them.

Add all of the ingredients to a large bowl and mix well. Enjoy!

ARIEL >

RED LENTIL DAAL

Packed full of flavor, every bite of this exotic dish will leave you feeling warm. This can be served as a thick soup or cooked a little bit longer to make a great addition to rice or quinoa.

1 tbsp (15 mL) olive oil

1 medium onion, diced small

1 tbsp (15 g) freshly grated ginger

1 tbsp (10 g) curry powder

½ tsp paprika

Pinch cayenne pepper

1 tsp sea salt

1½ cups (300 g) cooked lentils, drained and rinsed

1 small tomato, diced small

1 (14 oz [414 mL]) can full-fat coconut milk

1 cup (240 mL) purified water

Add the olive oil to a pot over medium heat, followed by the onion and ginger. Cook for 5 minutes until the onion becomes translucent, stirring often. Add the curry powder, paprika, cayenne and salt, and mix once more. Add the lentils, tomato, coconut milk and water. Bring to a boil, reduce heat and allow to simmer for 35–45 minutes until desired thickness is reached.

< SERENA

RAINBOW SLAW

SERVES 1—2

This isn't your normal coleslaw! Crunchy veggies with a tahini lemon dressing that brings on the cream and flavor, without all the added unhealthy stuff. This, by the way, is one salad that tastes amazing left to marinate and is great the next day.

SALAD

1½ cups (510 g) green cabbage, shredded

½ cup (170 g) purple cabbage, shredded

½ cup (55 g) carrot, grated

½ cup (75 g) red bell pepper, finely diced

½ cup (75 g) yellow or green bell pepper, finely diced

1 or 2 medium green onion stalks, diced

DRESSING

2 tbsp (30 g) tahini

2 tbsp (30 mL) olive oil

1½ tbsp (25 mL) fresh lemon juice

½ tsp sea salt

1 tbsp (15 mL) purified water, as needed

Save yourself some work grating and just use a sharp knife to slice the cabbage thin, cutting again in half to make sure it is in bite-size pieces. Add all of the veggies to a large bowl and toss.

Add the dressing ingredients to a small cup or bowl and whisk with a fork. Coat the salad with the dressing and mix well. Allow to marinate in the fridge or enjoy immediately.

LAURYN >

ROASTED TOMATO SOUP

MAKES 2 LARGE BOWLS OR 4 SMALL

Who knew that seven simple ingredients could create such delicious results? Tomatoes roasted with garlic and onion turn into a creamy, dreamy soup with a little love and basil.

10 medium tomatoes, cores removed and cut in half

1 medium white onion, cut into quarters

3 garlic cloves, peeled

⅓ cup (80 mL) olive oil

1½ tsp (8 g) sea salt

3 cups (710 mL) purified water

Large handful of basil

Preheat the oven to 400°F (200°C). Put the tomatoes, quartered onion and garlic on a rimmed baking tray. Cover the veggies with the oil and ½ teaspoon sea salt. Make sure they are evenly coated and that the tomatoes are face up. Put in the oven and bake for around 30 minutes or until the edges of the onions are caramelized.

When ready, remove from the oven and add everything to a medium-size pot. Add the water and 1 teaspoon of sea salt. Bring to a boil, stirring occasionally so it doesn't burn.

Reduce heat and allow to simmer for 20 minutes, stirring every 5 minutes. When ready, remove from heat and stir in the basil. Allow the soup to cool for a few minutes and use a hand blender to purée, making sure the blender is fully submerged so you don't get burned. If you don't have a hand mixer, allow to cool completely before putting the soup in your blender. Serve hot.

< ALLEGRA

CARROT GINGER SOUP

SERVES 2

This soup has coconut milk to thank for its rich and creamy deliciousness. And curry and fresh ginger to thank for its full flavor.

1 tbsp (15 mL) olive oil

3½–4 cups (450–515 g) carrots, diced

1 cup (150 g) white onion, diced

1 tbsp (15 g) fresh ginger, minced

1 tbsp (10 g) organic cane sugar

1½ tsp (5 g) curry powder

2 tsp (10 g) sea salt

2 cups (475 mL) purified water

1 (14 oz [414 mL]) can full-fat coconut milk, ¼ cup (60 mL) set aside for garnish

1 lime, optional garnish

Add the olive oil to a pot over medium heat, followed by the carrots, onion and ginger. Allow to gently simmer for 5 minutes, stirring occasionally so it does not stick.

Stir in the cane sugar, curry powder and sea salt. Add the water and allow to gently simmer for around 20 minutes, or until carrots are soft and you can cut through them easily.

Remove from heat and allow to cool for a few minutes. Add the can of coconut milk, making sure ¼ cup (60 mL) of it is set aside for garnish. Use your hand mixer to blend in the pot, making sure it is fully submerged so you don't burn yourself. If you do not have a hand mixer, allow ingredients to cool completely, then pour into your blender. Mix into a smooth purée and season with sea salt to taste.

Once blended, pour into bowls. Use a spoon to add a drizzle of coconut milk on top using a spoon, followed by a generous squeeze of lime juice, if you please.

DANI >

AVOCADO CAESAR

SERVES 1–2

Avocado and cherry tomatoes jazz up this fun take on a classic salad, and capers bring on the briny dressing. Just don't skimp on the garlic or you are missing out.

CROUTONS

1 or 2 pieces of gluten-free sliced bread

Olive oil

1 garlic clove, peeled and minced

Sea salt

DRESSING

⅓ cup (80 mL) olive oil

1½–2 tbsp (26-30 mL) fresh lemon juice

1 tbsp (10 g) capers

1 tbsp (10 g) fresh garlic, minced

½ tsp sea salt

½ tbsp (10 mL) purified water, as needed

SALAD

5 cups (275 g) romaine lettuce, ripped into bite-size pieces

2 tbsp (25 g) nutritional yeast, optional

10 cherry tomatoes, halved

1 small avocado, diced

Cut the bread into bite-size pieces. Coat a generous amount of olive oil in a frying pan over medium-low heat and add the bread and garlic to it. Mix it around so the bread is coated in oil and cook for a few minutes until it becomes fragrant and golden-brown underneath. Flip and cook the other side, adding more oil if needed. Cook until golden-brown as well and remove from heat and set aside. Season with some sea salt.

To make the dressing, add all of the ingredients to your blender and mix until smooth and creamy. Dressing should be quite thick but add ½ tablespoon (10 mL) of water if needed. Put the lettuce into a big bowl, add the dressing and toss well. Add the nutritional yeast and mix once more. Throw in the cherry tomatoes and croutons and toss again, adding the avocado on top in wedges as garnish. Enjoy!

< TAYLOR

BLACK BEAN SOUP

MAKES 4 BOWLS

Beans, beans, good for the heart! This soup is hearty indeed, chock-full of black beans and fresh veggies. Spice it up with some jalapeños and cilantro if you choose. If you find it a bit too thick after blending, just add a few spoonfuls of water.

2 ears of fresh corn, sliced off the cob

1 tbsp (15 mL) olive oil

1 cup (150 g) white onion, diced

2 tsp (10 g) sea salt

1 tsp cumin

1 tsp paprika

⅛ tsp cayenne pepper

3 cups (720 g) canned black beans, drained and rinsed

3 medium tomatoes, diced

2½ cups (590 mL) purified water

1 small avocado, cut in wedges

1 or 2 green onion stalks

Put ¼ of the fresh corn aside for garnish. Add the olive oil and onion to a large saucepan. Cook over medium-low heat for around 5 minutes, until the onion becomes translucent, stirring frequently. Add the salt, cumin, paprika and cayenne and mix. Throw in the beans, tomatoes and corn and allow to gently simmer for 5–10 minutes until liquid begins to form.

Add the water and turn up the heat slightly to bring to a boil. Once it begins to boil, turn the heat back down and allow to gently simmer for around 20 minutes, stirring it every 5 minutes or so.

When ready, remove from heat and allow to cool for a few minutes. Use your hand blender to mix it well, making sure it is fully submerged so the soup doesn't splatter. Serve in bowls, adding some avocado, green onion and corn for garnish. If you have any black beans leftover, you can also add a sprinkle of them on top, if you please.

HONOR >

GAZPACHO FRESCA

MAKES 2–4 BOWLS

The Spaniards were onto something when they invented gazpacho. Just add a few simple ingredients to your blender, strain it, chill and voilà! You've got a delicious fresh soup jam-packed with goodness.

SOUP

5 very ripe medium tomatoes, core removed

1 medium red pepper, core removed

½ cup (75 g) white onion, diced

1 cucumber, peeled

1 cup (40 g) fresh basil leaves

2 tbsp (30 mL) olive oil

2 tbsp (30 mL) apple cider vinegar

1 tbsp (15 mL) fresh lemon juice

1 tsp sea salt

OPTIONAL GARNISH

Extra diced tomatoes

Extra diced onions

Extra basil leaves

Add all the soup ingredients to your blender and mix well. It may help to dice all of the veggies first to make it easier to mix.

When fully blended, pass through a fine strainer to remove all of the pulp, using the back of a spoon to push it through. Discard the pulp and chill in the refrigerator for one hour before enjoying. Garnish with diced tomatoes, onion and basil, if you please.

< KATE

SHREDDED KALE SALAD

SERVES 1—2

This is a delicious way to enjoy one of the healthiest leafy greens. Little bites of kale are marinated in a creamy tahini dressing and topped with crunchy sunflower seeds.

DRESSING

¼ cup (60 g) tahini

1½ tbsp (25 mL) tamari

½ tbsp (10 mL) apple cider vinegar

½ tsp freshly grated ginger

1-2 tbsp (15-30 mL) purified water, as needed

SALAD

3 cups (50 g) packed kale, stems removed

¼ cup (35 g) raw unsalted sunflower seeds

1 cup (170 g) purple cabbage, diced small

½ cup (55 g) grated carrot

½ cup (75 g) red bell pepper

Use a fork to whisk all of the dressing ingredients together in a small cup. Add 1 or 2 tablespoons (15-30 mL) of water as needed. The dressing should be thick and creamy, but not paste-like.

Roll chunks of kale together and use a knife to cut them into small pieces. Add them to a bowl and pour half of the dressing on top. Use a rubber spatula or your hands to really mix it well and massage the dressing into the kale.

Toast the sunflower seeds. Put them in a small pan over medium-high heat and give them a shake often so they do not burn. Wait around 2 minutes until they start to brown, and give them another moment to ensure they are done evenly. Remove from heat and set aside.

Add the rest of the veggies to the kale and pour the rest of the dressing over them. Use a rubber spatula; you won't want to miss a drop of the dressing. Mix well, then and add the sunflower seeds and mix once more.

JENNY >

ENSALADA MEXICANA

SERVES 1–2

Even non-salad eaters will enjoy this one. Nachos just make everything more fun. Feel free to double the amount of jalapeño if you like things extra spicy.

DRESSING

¼ cup (60 mL) olive oil

¼ medium, very ripe avocado

2 tbsp (30 mL) fresh lime juice

1 jalapeño, finely chopped

1 tbsp (15 mL) apple cider vinegar

1 tbsp (10 g) blonde coconut nectar

½ tsp sea salt

SALAD

5 cups (235 g) loosely packed romaine lettuce, ripped into bite-size pieces

¾ medium very ripe avocado, diced

½ cup (75 g) red pepper, finely diced

1 medium tomato, finely diced

1 cup (185 g) cooked black beans, drained and rinsed

1 green onion stalk, finely chopped

Cilantro, finely chopped, for an optional garnish

A few handfuls of plain, salted nacho chips (gluten-free)

Use your hand blender or a small food processor to mix all of the dressing ingredients. Blend well.

Put the lettuce in a large bowl. Pour half the dressing over the lettuce and toss well. Sprinkle avocado, red pepper and tomatoes on top, followed by the black beans and green onion. Add cilantro, or extra diced jalapeño, if you please.

Drizzle a generous amount of the dressing and crumble a few handfuls of nachos on top. Enjoy!

< REBECCA

SUNSHINE SALAD

The more colors a salad has, the more fun it is to eat. With a rainbow of fresh veggies and a creamy avocado lemon dressing, what fun you will have with this one indeed.

SALAD

1 medium or large avocado, diced

5 cups (275 g) romaine lettuce

1 cup (150 g) cherry tomatoes, quartered

½ cup (35 g) purple cabbage, shredded

½ cup (75 g) yellow bell pepper, diced

¼ cup (35 g) cucumber, diced

5 or 6 oil packed sundried tomatoes, diced

Sunflower sprouts to garnish, optional

DRESSING

¼ cup (60 g) avocado

½ cup (20 g) fresh basil

¼ cup (60 mL) olive oil

2 tbsp (30 mL) fresh lemon juice

½ tsp sea salt

1-2 tbsp (15-30 mL) purified water, as needed

Scoop ¼ cup (60 g) from the avocado and set it aside for the dressing. Put the lettuce on a big plate and pile the rest of the veggies on top.

Put all of the dressing ingredients in the blender and mix. Add 1 tablespoon (15 mL) of water if needed. Dressing should be thick and creamy. Pour on top of the salad and enjoy.

ELINE >

SWEET TREATS

I saved the sweetest chapter for last! Because *LBCB*'s beginnings started with dessert, I will always have a soft spot (and sweet tooth) for treats.

Some of these recipes are on the healthier side, with no added sugar, and others are sinfully sweet. There really is no sugarcoating sugar, but when you are busy filling up on so many other veggies, it's okay to have a little bit of fun, so enjoy!

FREEZER FUDGE

Mmmmm, chocolate. Rich and creamy, this delicious treat only takes minutes to whip up. The only downside of course is waiting for it to freeze.

1 cup (170 g) organic dark chocolate
¼ cup (60 mL) vegan milk
¼ cup (25 g) cacao
¼ cup (60 mL) pure maple syrup

Melt the chocolate with the vegan milk in a small saucepan over medium heat. Stir often with a rubber spatula so it does not stick to the bottom. When melted, remove from heat and add the cacao and maple syrup. Mix well. Pour into a small 4–5 inch (10–12.5 cm) container and place in the freezer for a few hours to set. Store in the freezer until ready to serve. Cut into small squares before eating.

MONTY >

STRAWBERRY COCONUT ICE POPS

MAKES 3 OR 4

Satisfy your sweet tooth without going overboard with this light, easy-to-make treat.

½ cup (75 g) strawberries, stems removed

¾ cup (180 mL) canned, full-fat coconut milk

1 tbsp (15 mL) coconut nectar

1 tbsp (15 mL) fresh lime juice

In a blender, mix the strawberries, ½ cup (120 mL) coconut milk and coconut nectar into a smooth liquid. In a small bowl, mix the lime juice and ¼ cup (60 mL) coconut milk.

Fill each ice pop mold ⅓ of the way full with the strawberry mixture. Slowly pour the lime mixture evenly into each mold on top of the strawberry to create another layer. Top each one off with the rest of the strawberry. Put in the freezer overnight or for at least 4 hours.

When frozen and ready to remove, you can run lukewarm water on the tip of each mold to help gently loosen it without breaking.

< LAUREN + PAO

COOKIES AND CREAM SANDWICHES

MAKES 10

Cookies and cream are two things that just belong together, especially if it's in the form of a sandwich. And when the sandwich is two soft no-bake chocolate cookies, and a creamy peanut butter filling, then it is really meant to be.

COOKIE

1½ cups (150 g) almond meal

½ cup (120 mL) pure maple syrup

⅓ cup (35 g) cacao

3 tbsp (45 mL) extra-virgin coconut oil, melted

¼ tsp sea salt

CREAM

1 cup (110 g) raw unsalted cashews

¼ cup (60 mL) extra-virgin coconut oil, melted

¼ cup (60 mL) pure maple syrup

2 tbsp (25 g) smooth natural peanut butter

2 tbsp (30 mL) purified water

1 tsp natural vanilla extract

¼ cup (45 g) organic dark chocolate chips

Line a bread tin with parchment paper. Mix the cookie ingredients in your food processor. Take half the dough, cover and put it aside, keeping it at room temperature. Put the other half in the bottom of the bread tin, using a rubber spatula to evenly distribute.

To make the cream, put the cashews in the food processor and blend them into a powder. Add the coconut oil and blend once more. Add the maple syrup, peanut butter, water and vanilla and mix until it forms a thick dough. Mix in the chocolate chips by hand and use a rubber spatula to distribute on top of the cookie layer in the bread tin. Put in the freezer for an hour or so.

Once the peanut butter layer is hardened, add the remaining cookie dough, once again using your rubber spatula to distribute. Put back in the freezer for 4 hours to freeze completely. When ready, remove and cut into squares. Store in the freezer.

CLAUDIA >

CHOCOLATE PEANUT BUTTER TARTS

MAKES 9 SQUARES

A crunchy peanut crust topped with a creamy peanut butter fudge are the perfect match in this *LBCB* classic.

CRUST

2 cups (320 g) roasted unsalted peanuts

¼ tsp sea salt

¼ cup (60 g) extra-virgin coconut oil, at room temperature

¼ cup (60 mL) pure maple syrup

FUDGE

1 cup (180 g) organic dark chocolate chips

⅓ cup (80 mL) pure maple syrup

½ tbsp (8 mL) vanilla extract, optional

1 cup (180 g) smooth peanut butter

Put the peanuts and salt in the food processor and grind into a coarse powder. You can leave some chunks if you want it to be a bit crunchy. Add the coconut oil and maple syrup and pulse again until a dough is formed. Remove from the food processor and press into the bottom of a 9-inch (23 cm) square casserole or pie dish. Use a spatula or the back of a spoon to smooth it out. Put in the freezer to set.

Melt the chocolate chips in a saucepan over medium-low heat. Make sure that water does not come in contact with the pan or chocolate or it will not melt properly. Add the maple syrup and vanilla and mix thoroughly. Remove from heat and add the peanut butter. You can mix it completely, or leave some of it unmixed to create a marble effect. Pour over top of the crust, spreading it evenly with a rubber spatula and place back in the freezer for an hour or two to set.

When ready, remove from the freezer and cut into squares. Serve chilled and store in the freezer or refrigerator.

< KATE

BANANA POPS

MAKES 6

This is a fun, easy treat you can indulge in. Almost guilt-free to boot!

2 medium bananas, not overly ripe
¼ cup (45 g) smooth or crunchy almond butter
1 cup (180 g) organic dark chocolate chips
1 tbsp (15 g) extra-virgin coconut oil
Crushed pecans, to coat

Cut the banana into 3-inch (7.5 cm) sections. Insert an ice pop stick a little more than halfway into each one. Place on a large plate lined with parchment paper and put in the freezer for two or three hours to harden. Depending on how oily your almond butter is, you may want to put it in the freezer for 10–30 minutes before you use it, just give it a stir first.

When the bananas are frozen, remove them from the freezer. Try to avoid handling them with their sticks. Spread a layer of almond butter over the sides of each piece, avoiding the top and bottom. Once messily coated, you can smooth it out by holding it at the top and bottom with your thumb and forefinger. Drag the knife around the sides, while rotating the banana. Put back in freezer for 30 minutes.

Five minutes before you remove the bananas from the freezer, melt the chocolate chips and coconut oil over low heat. Stir with a spatula until melted and remove from heat and allow to cool for a few minutes. Make sure water does not come in contact with chocolate or your utensils or it will not melt properly. Add the crushed pecans to a small plate and set aside.

Remove the bananas from the freezer and use the spatula or a spoon to cover them with chocolate. Roll it in the pecans or sprinkle them on top when it is still wet. Allow to dry for a few seconds before placing back on the plate.

Freeze for another 30 minutes to set. Best served frozen, but also taste great mushy!

CAILIN >

MOJITO CUPCAKES

MAKES 12

This recipe is all the fun of a mojito in the form of a cupcake. Fresh lime and mint go oh so perfectly together in this one. Don't skimp on the quality of the all-purpose gluten-free flour you buy, and make sure to add xanthan gum if it calls for it.

CUPCAKES

2 cups (250 g) all-purpose gluten-free flour blend

1 cup (190 g) organic cane sugar

1½ tbsp (2 g) fresh mint, finely chopped

1½ tsp baking soda

½ tsp sea salt

1 cup (240 mL) purified water

½ cup (120 mL) grapeseed oil

2 tbsp (30 mL) apple cider vinegar

2 tbsp (30 mL) fresh lime juice

1 tsp fresh lime zest

FROSTING

¾ cup (180 g) coconut butter, stirred before use

⅓ cup (80 mL) coconut nectar

1 tbsp (15 mL) fresh lime juice

½ tsp fresh lime zest

2–5 tbsp (30-75 mL) purified water, as needed

Preheat the oven to 350°F (175°C). Line a cupcake tray with 12 liners.

Add the flour, sugar, baking soda, mint and sea salt to a large bowl and sift well with a fork. Add the water, oil, vinegar, lime juice and zest and mix well until there are no clumps.

Pour ¼ cup (60 mL) of batter into each cupcake liner so they are evenly distributed. There may be a little batter left over. Put the cupcakes in the oven for 15–20 minutes, removing once you can poke a fork or toothpick into the center of them and it comes out clean.

In the meantime, make the frosting by adding all ingredients except the water to your food processor and mix. Use a rubber spatula to scrape down the sides. Add 1 tablespoon (15 mL) of water at a time until it becomes smooth and creamy as desired. Coconut butter hardens when chilled, so leave at room temperature before frosting.

Remove the cupcakes from the oven when ready and transfer from the cupcake tray onto a cooling rack or plate. Allow to cool before frosting.

< SAYA

PECAN PIE BALLS

MAKES 12

Everything you could ask for in a pecan pie all rolled into one little bite—with a chocolate coating as an added bonus.

DOUGH

1½ cups (150 g) raw unsalted pecans

¾ cup (110 g) juicy Thompson raisins

2 tbsp (30 mL) vegan milk

2 tbsp (30 g) extra-virgin coconut oil

1 tsp cinnamon

CHOCOLATE SAUCE

½ cup (85 g) organic dark chocolate

½ tbsp (8 g) coconut oil

Make the dough by adding the pecans to your food processor and mixing into a coarse powder, making sure there are no large chunks left. Add the raisins, milk, coconut oil and cinnamon and blend again until smooth.

Cover a plate with parchment paper. Drop 12 small, even spoonfuls of the dough onto the parchment paper and place in the freezer for 10 minutes to set.

Remove the dough from the freezer and roll each spoonful into a small ball in the palm of your hand. If they are too sticky to work with, place back in the freezer for a few more minutes. Store in the freezer once more when finished rolling.

To make the chocolate sauce, melt the chocolate and coconut oil in a saucepan over medium-low heat. Use a rubber spatula to stir constantly, making sure it doesn't stick. Make sure water does not come in contact with the chocolate or your utensils or it will not melt properly. When melted, remove and transfer to a small bowl. Allow to cool for one minute. Get out a fork, spoon and place a fresh piece of parchment paper on a plate.

Remove the dough from the freezer and place the balls one at a time in the chocolate sauce. Use the spoon to cover each one with sauce and a fork to gently remove them. Place each one on the new parchment paper and put back into the freezer to set for 1 or 2 hours.

Store in the fridge or freezer; best served cold.

GEMMA >

BANANA MAPLE CREAM PIE

FILLS A 9-INCH (23 CM) PIE DISH

This dreamy pie has fresh banana over a crunchy pecan crust and a thick, creamy filling. Try it with a dash of Coconut Whipped Cream on top.

CRUST

2 cups (200 g) raw unsalted pecans

¼ cup (60 mL) pure maple syrup

¼ cup (60 mL) extra-virgin coconut oil, melted

½ tsp cinnamon

1 medium banana

FILLING

1 cup (110 g) raw unsalted cashews

½ cup (115 g) banana, mashed

¼ cup (60 mL) extra-virgin coconut oil, melted

¼ cup (60 mL) pure maple syrup

OPTIONAL GARNISH

Extra banana slices

Coconut Whipped Cream (page 188)

For the crust, add all ingredients (except the banana) to your food processor and pulse until the pecans are broken down into small pieces. Remove from the food processor, making sure the coconut oil and maple syrup are evenly mixed, then press into the bottom of a 9-inch (23 cm) square casserole or pie dish. Use a spatula or the back of a spoon to smooth it out, leaving the sides slightly higher than the rest to form the crust. Chop the banana into ⅛-inch (3 mm) discs and evenly place in the pie base.

To make the cream filling, add the cashews to your food processor and blend into a coarse powder. Add the rest of the ingredients and blend until smooth and creamy. Remove from the processor and pour over the bananas, filling the crust. Put in the freezer or fridge for an hour or so to set. Keep cold until ready to serve, and garnish with extra banana slices and Coconut Whipped Cream, if you please.

< STEPHANIE

APPLE CARAMEL TARTS

FILLS AN 8-INCH (20 CM) PIE OR CASSEROLE DISH

Forget what you know about apple tarts and try this easy no-bake version. Maple syrup and cinnamon add full flavor to fresh, crisp apples. Choose a more tart-flavored apple for best results.

FILLING

2 or 3 apples, diced

½ tbsp (8 mL) fresh lemon juice

1 tsp cinnamon

2 tbsp (30 mL) pure maple syrup

CRUST

2 cups (315 g) wheat-free rolled oats

2 cups (300 g) dried pitted dates

¼ cup (60 mL) pure maple syrup

¼ cup (60 mL) extra-virgin coconut oil, melted

½ tsp sea salt

CARAMEL

1 cup (150 g) dried pitted dates

½ cup (120 mL) vegan milk

2 tbsp (30 mL) pure maple syrup

Add all filling ingredients to a bowl and mix well. Allow these ingredients to marinate while making the rest.

Make the crust by grinding the oats in your food processor into a coarse powder. Add the dates and blend until they begin to break down. Add the maple syrup, coconut oil and sea salt and blend into a thick, doughy paste. Use a rubber spatula to scrape down the sides of your processor if you need to. Remove from the processor and press evenly into the bottom of an 8-inch (20 cm) pie or casserole dish.

To make the caramel, add the dates to the food processor and blend until they break down. Add the milk and blend once more into a liquid. Add the maple syrup and blend for a few minutes until smooth and creamy. Pour over the apples and mix well.

Pour the apple mixture on top of the crust and evenly distribute. Put in the freezer to set for an hour or so. Cut into squares before eating and store in the freezer or refrigerator.

JENNY >

CASHEW COOKIE DOUGH

MAKES AROUND 2 CUPS (500 G)

Just like the real thing, minus the uncooked flour. I just keep mine in the freezer with a spoon in the bowl, making it easier to go back for more sneaky bites.

1 cup (110 g) raw unsalted cashews

¼ cup (60 mL) pure maple syrup

¼ cup (60 mL) extra-virgin coconut oil, melted or softened

1 tsp natural vanilla extract

½ tsp cinnamon

⅓ cup (60 g) organic dark chocolate chips

Put the cashews in your food processor and pulse into a coarse powder. Add the maple syrup, coconut oil, vanilla and cinnamon and blend once more into a dough. Use a rubber spatula to scrape down the sides of your processor on occasion. Add the chocolate chips and pulse only a few times, so they remain in chunks.

Remove from the food processor and put into a small bowl. Put in the freezer for 2 hours to harden. Store in the freezer.

< ANDREA

CHAI LATTE CUPCAKES

MAKES 12

Perfectly fluffy and moist, these babies have a hint of chai paired with a mouth-watering dark chocolate frosting. Sold? Make sure you use a quality all-purpose gluten-free flour mix and add xanthan gum if the flour calls for it.

CUPCAKES

1 cup (240 mL) purified water

4 chai tea bags

2 cups (250 g) gluten-free flour

1 cup (200 g) organic cane sugar

1 tsp baking soda

½ tsp cinnamon

½ tsp sea salt

½ cup (120 mL) grapeseed oil

1½ tbsp (25 mL) apple cider vinegar

1 tsp pure vanilla extract

FROSTING

½ cup (95 g) organic dark chocolate

¼ cup (60 mL) vegan milk

2 tbsp (30 mL) pure maple syrup

Boil the water in a small saucepan. When it begins to bubble, add the tea bags and allow them to steep for 15 minutes or so. Use a spoon to push on the bags to help them steep more. When ready, remove from the pot, and once again use the spoon to press them against the side of the pot to remove all of the liquid. Measure out the liquid again and add more water so it equals 1 cup (240 mL).

While the tea is steeping, preheat the oven to 350°F (175°C). Line a muffin tray with 12 liners. Add the flour, sugar, baking soda, cinnamon and sea salt to a large mixing bowl and sift well with a fork. Add the tea-soaked water, grapeseed oil, apple cider vinegar and vanilla. Mix once more until a dough forms.

Put ¼ cup (60 mL) scoops of batter into each cupcake liner. There may be a little bit left over, don't fill the liners to the top. Put in the oven to bake for 17–21 minutes. Keep a close eye on them near the end as all gluten-free flours can give different results. You know they're ready when the cupcakes are slightly golden on top and a toothpick or fork can be poked through the center and comes out clean.

To make the frosting, heat all of the ingredients in a small saucepan over medium-low heat, using a rubber spatula to make sure it doesn't stick to the bottom. Once the chocolate is melted, transfer mixture to a small bowl and set aside until the cupcakes have cooled. Frost the cupcakes when ready to eat.

TONYA + NATALIE >

STRAWBERRY CREAMCAKE

FILLS A 9-INCH (23 CM) PIE DISH

This creamy strawberry cake tastes much more decadent than you think it would, considering how easy it is to make. Simplicity wins again! If you don't have shredded coconut, just use extra almond meal instead.

CRUST

¾ cup (110 g) dates

½ cup (60 g) almond meal

¼ cup (20 g) shredded unsweetened coconut

¼ cup (60 mL) extra-virgin coconut oil, melted or softened

Pinch sea salt

FILLING

2 cups (225 g) raw unsalted cashews

½ cup (120 mL) extra-virgin coconut oil, melted or softened

⅓ cup (65 g) blonde coconut nectar

2 tbsp (30 mL) fresh lemon juice

½ tsp natural vanilla extract

2 tbsp (30 mL) purified water

½ cup (75 g) fresh strawberries

GARNISH

4 or 5 strawberries, stems removed and cut in half

Fresh mint, optional

Coconut Whipped Cream (page 188), optional

Add the dates, almond meal and shredded coconut to your food processor and blend until the dates break down to small chunks. Add the coconut oil and salt and blend until a dough forms. You may need to scrape down the sides of your food processor on occasion with a rubber spatula. Remove mixture from the food processor and place in the bottom of a 9-inch (23 cm) pie or casserole dish. Use your fingers to even it out.

To make the filling, add the cashews to the processor and blend into a coarse powder. Add the coconut oil, coconut nectar, lemon juice, vanilla and water and blend into a cream. Once again, you may need to scrape down the sides with a rubber spatula. Add the strawberries and blend once more until there are no chunks left. Pour on top of the crust and use the spatula to even it out. Put in the freezer for 2 hours to harden. Cut into slices and store in the freezer or refrigerator until ready to serve. Garnish with strawberries, Coconut Whipped Cream and mint, if you please.

< ZOE

CAROB BARS

MAKES 4 SQUARES

Have some fun without the sugar with this treat that's sweetened naturally. Want it just slightly sweet? Skip the Stevia and add a tablespoon or two (15–30 mL) of coconut nectar.

¼ cup (50 g) carob powder

¼ cup (60 g) extra virgin coconut oil, melted or softened

¼ cup (45 g) smooth or crunchy almond butter

½ tsp natural vanilla extract

¼ tsp cinnamon

15 drops of liquid stevia

1 cup (20 g) crispy rice cereal

Add all of the ingredients except the rice cereal to a medium-size bowl and mix well. When mixed, stir in the cereal. Add to a small 4- or 5-inch (10–12.5 cm) container, then use a rubber spatula to even it out and put in the freezer for 20 minutes to set. Store in the fridge or refrigerator until ready to eat.

SARAH >

HOT CHOCOLATE COOKIES

MAKES 12 COOKIES

Double the chocolate with a hint of spice makes this decadent treat a fun spin on a not-so-average cookie.

1 cup (125 g) all-purpose gluten-free flour mix

½ cup (100 g) organic cane sugar

¼ cup (25 g) organic cacao

½ tsp baking soda

⅛ tsp cayenne pepper

⅛ tsp sea salt

¼ cup (60 mL) grapeseed oil

3 tbsp (45 mL) pure maple syrup

2 tbsp (30 mL) vegan milk

½ tsp natural vanilla

¼ cup (45 g) organic dark chocolate chips

Preheat the oven to 350°F (175°C). Lightly grease a cookie sheet with oil. Be sure to double check if your gluten-free flour requires xanthan gum and add the appropriate amount if so.

Add the flour, cane sugar, cacao, baking soda, cayenne and sea salt to a large bowl and sift with a fork. Stir in the oil, maple syrup, milk and vanilla and mix once more. Stir in the chocolate chips.

Take small pieces of dough and roll into 1-inch (2.5 cm) balls in the palms of your hands. Place on the cookie sheet, evenly spaced apart as they will expand.

Put in the oven and bake for 9–11 minutes. They may seem not finished when you remove them, but they will crisp up a lot as they cool. Allow to cool for a minute or two on the cookie sheet then transfer to a cooling rack.

< ARIEL

COCO–CHOCO MACAROONS

MAKES 12

Have you tried coconut butter yet? Here is the perfect way to get on it with these delicious macaroons filled with an extra dose of chocolate.

¼ cup (60 g) coconut butter, stirred well before using

¼ cup (65 mL) pure maple syrup

½ tsp natural vanilla extract

1 cup (75 g) unsweetened shredded coconut

¼ cup (45 g) dark chocolate chips

Preheat oven to 350°F (175°C). Place a piece of parchment paper on a baking sheet.

Add the coconut butter, maple syrup and vanilla to a large bowl and mix well. Add the shredded coconut and chocolate and mix once more. Take spoonfuls of the dough, and drop it onto the baking sheet to form 12 equal pieces.

Bake for around 5 minutes, or until they are slightly golden-brown on the bottom. Leave to cool for at least 30 minutes on baking sheet so they can harden and set. Store in an airtight container at room temperature.

ANIA >

OATMEAL RAISIN BITES

MAKES 10

Everyone's favorite comforting combo brought to you in a little no-bake bite.

1 cup (80 g) wheat-free rolled oats

⅓ cup (75 g) extra-virgin coconut oil, softened or melted

¼ cup (60 mL) pure maple syrup

¼ cup (60 g) smooth or crunchy almond butter

⅛ cup (20 g) raisins, chopped

½ tsp cinnamon

¼ tsp vanilla extract

Put the oats in a food processor and pulse for a few seconds. Do not grind into a powder, just make sure they are coarsely chopped. If you do not have a food processor, use a large knife to chop them more finely.

Add to a large bowl with the rest of the ingredients and mix well with a rubber spatula.

Put in freezer for 10 minutes to slightly harden. Remove from freezer and roll into 10 balls in the palm of your hand, and put back in the freezer to harden more. Serve cold and store in the fridge or freezer.

< GURINA

COCONUT WHIPPED CREAM

MAKES 1 CUP (240 ML)

Layer it on pancakes, top it on smoothies or eat it straight from the jar. Whatever you decide, this quick and easy treat will be a welcoming addition to just about anything. Not all brands make for good coconut cream, so check online for the ones available to you.

1 (14 oz [414 mL-]) can full-fat coconut milk (stored in the fridge overnight—do not shake)

1 tbsp (15 mL) coconut nectar

½ tsp pure vanilla extract, optional

Remove the coconut milk from the fridge and gently open the can. Use a spoon to scoop up the top creamy part that should have hardened, being careful to leave the water in the can below. Put the creamy top part into a large mixing bowl and add the coconut nectar and vanilla. Use a whisk attachment on an electric hand mixer to whisk the ingredients into a light fluff. Store in the fridge until ready to serve.

VIKKI >

TIPS
+ TRICKS

I highly recommend using fresh, local or organic ingredients as much as possible; it really makes a difference in quality. On a budget? Scope out farmers' markets, stock up on dry ingredients in bulk, do some online shopping or see if your neighborhood has a local co-op.

It's always good to purchase cacao, chocolate, sweeteners and sugar organically so you know that they were made in a safe way for the environment and the people harvesting them. Most liquid sweeteners can be interchanged. I like to use blonde coconut nectar when I need something light and maple syrup for everything else—I am Canadian after all! Try to buy coconut nectar organically and from a renewable source to protect those beautiful coconut trees. For maple syrup, always buy the pure kind and stay away from the knockoffs using corn syrup or fructose.

For vegan milk, I prefer unsweetened almond milk as it is the thickest for smoothies. Certain brands of rice milk can also be great, and for a creamier taste, coconut milk in the carton works great too. Just stay away from soy and its icky side effects. When buying coconut milk in the can, make sure that it is just straight-up coconut, the ones marked as light or low fat have water added to them. And we don't want our coconut milk less creamy do we!?!

When I have time, I try to soak raw cashews for a few hours before using them. This removes the toxic enzymes that protect them, making them much easier to digest, as well as much easier for your food processor to blend them into something thick and creamy. Just make sure you rinse them well first.

As for tahini, I always buy the lighter beige one. The darker versions have a much stronger taste and can be overbearing a lot of the time, especially if you are only using it to thicken the texture in a sauce. Unless of course you really love tahini that much, then go for it.

And last but not least, buy your coconut oil extra virgin, tamari wheat-free, apple cider vinegar unrefined and you should be all set!

ACKNOWLEDGMENTS

Thanks to my mom for all her support, my dad for all his help, Peggi for always being there and Juan for everything and anything.

Thank you to all of my old and new friends who let me take their portraits for this book.

A special thanks to Will and Marissa at Page Street Publishing for this amazing opportunity. And to Meg for her amazing design skills.

ABOUT THE AUTHOR

Jessica Milan is a photographer and foodie from Toronto.

INDEX

apples
    Apple Caramel Tarts, 172
    Detoxer, The, 30
    Drink Your Greens, 37
asparagus
    Pasta Primavera, 58
    Veggie Tempura, 122
avocados
    Avocado Caesar, 143
    Black Bean Burrito, 62
    Black Bean Soup, 144
    California Wrap, 74
    Chickpea "Omelette", 95
    Chunky Guacamole, 114
    Ensalada Mexicana, 151
    Fiesta Layer Dip, 102
    Summer Rolls, 109
    Sunshine Salad, 152
    Tex-Mex Potato Skins, 54
    Veggie Quesadillas, 83

bananas
    Acai Blast, 13
    Almond Date Smoothie, 26
    Banana Acai Bowl, 91
    Banana Maple Cream Pie, 171
    Banana Pops, 164
    Berry Blaster, 21
    Blue Melon, 25
    Double Fudge Shake, 18
    Fully Loaded Pancakes, 92
    Key Lime Smoothie, 38
    Peaches + Cream, 29
    Raspberry Frostie, 17
    Stracciatella Shake, 14
    Sunrise Smoothie, 34
    Tropi-Green Smoothie, 22
black beans
    Black Bean Burrito, 62
    Black Bean Soup, 144
    Ensalada Mexicana, 151
    Fiesta Layer Dip, 102
    Tex-Mex Potato Skins, 54
blueberries
    Acai Blast, 13
    Blueberry Lemon Jonnycakes, 96
    Blue Melon, 25
broccoli
    Tahini Rice Bowl, 69
    Veggie Pad Thai, 46
Brussels sprouts. See Veggie Fried
    Rice, 73

cabbage
    Rainbow Slaw, 136
    Shredded Kale Salad, 148
    Sunshine Salad, 152
    Tahini Greens, 128
    Veggie Fried Rice, 73
carrots
    Carrot Ginger Soup, 140
    Rainbow Slaw, 136
    Shredded Kale Salad, 148
    Summer Rolls, 109

cauliflower. See Cauliflower
    "Couscous," 132
Chai Latte Cupcakes, 176
chickpeas
    Chickpea "Omelette", 95
    Hummus, 110
    Moroccan Soup, 131
    Quinoa Yam Patties, 49
chocolate
    Banana Pops, 164
    Cashew Cookie Dough, 175
    Chai Latte Cupcakes, 176
    Chocolate Peanut Butter Tarts, 163
    Coco-Choco Macaroons, 184
    Cookies and Cream Sandwiches, 160
    Double Fudge Shake, 18
    Freezer Fudge, 156
    Fully Loaded Pancakes, 92
    Hot Chocolate Cookies, 183
    Pecan Pie Balls, 168
    Stracciatella Shake, 14
coconut butter
    Coco-Choco Macaroons, 184
    Mojito Cupcakes, 167
coconut ice cream. See Stracciatella
    Shake, 14
coconut milk
    Carrot Ginger Soup, 140
    Coconut Curry on Rice, 50
    Coconut Whipped Cream, 188
    Orange Mango Lassi, 10
    Red Lentil Daal, 135
    Strawberry Coconut Ice Pops, 159
    Sweet Chili Soba, 57
coconut, shredded
    Coco-Choco Macaroons, 184
    Strawberry Creamcake, 179
    Strawberry Cream Pancakes, 87
coconut water. See Tropi-Green
    Smoothie, 22
coconut yogurt. See Berry Parfait, 88
corn
    Black Bean Soup, 144
    Perfect Popcorn, 113
corn tortillas
    California Wrap, 74
    Veggie Quesadillas, 83
corn tostadas. See Fajitas Tostadas, 45
cucumber
    Black Bean Burrito, 62
    California Wrap, 74
    Cauliflower "Couscous," 132
    Chunky Guacamole, 114
    Cucumber Cups, 121
    Drink Your Greens, 37
    Gazpacho Fresca, 147
    Summer Rolls, 109
    Sunshine Salad, 152

dates
    Almond Date Smoothie, 26
    Apple Caramel Tarts, 172
    Strawberry Creamcake, 179

eggplant. See Roasted Ratatouille, 65

grapefruit. See Citrus Zinger, 33

kale
    Shredded Kale Salad, 148
    Tahini Greens, 128
kidney beans. See Sweet Potato Chili, 61

lentils. See Red Lentil Daal, 135
lettuce
    Avocado Caesar, 143
    Ensalada Mexicana, 151
    Fiesta Layer Dip, 102
    Sunshine Salad, 152
    Tahini Greens, 128

mango. See Orange Mango Lassi, 10
melon. See Blue Melon, 25
mixed fruit
    Banana Acai Bowl, 91
    Berry Blaster, 21
    Berry Parfait, 88
    Fruit Salad, 99

oats
    Apple Caramel Tarts, 172
    Banana Acai Bowl, 91
    Mornin' Oats, 80
    Oatmeal Raisin Bites, 187
olives. See Cauliflower "Couscous," 132
oranges
    Citrus Zinger, 33
    Orange Mango Lassi, 10
    Sunrise Smoothie, 34

papaya. See Tropi-Green Smoothie, 22
pasta
    Pasta Primavera, 58
    Speedy Cheezy Pasta, 70
    Sun-Dried Tomato Pasta Pesto, 66
peaches. See Peaches + Cream, 29
pineapple. See Citrus Zinger, 33
potatoes
    Tex-Mex Potato Skins, 54
    Zucchini Fritters, 84

quinoa
    Quinoa Yam Patties, 49
    Stuffed Red Peppers, 42
    Zesty Quinoa Bowl, 77

raisins
    Oatmeal Raisin Bites, 187
    Pecan Pie Balls, 168
raspberries. See Raspberry Frostie, 17
rice
    Carob Bars, 180
    Coconut Curry on Rice, 50
    Tahini Rice Bowl, 69
    Veggie Fried Rice, 73

snow peas. See Pasta Primavera, 58

soba noodles. See Sweet Chili Soba, 57
spinach
    California Wrap, 74
    Chickpea "Omelette", 95
    Detoxer, The, 30
    Drink Your Greens, 37
    Tahini Rice Bowl, 69
    Tropi-Green Smoothie, 22
strawberries
    Berry Parfait, 88
    Strawberry Coconut Ice Pops, 159
    Strawberry Creamcake, 179
    Strawberry Cream Pancakes, 87
    Sunrise Smoothie, 34
sweet potatoes
    Quinoa Yam Patties, 49
    Sweet Potato Chili, 61
    Sweet Potato Coins, 118
    Zesty Quinoa Bowl, 77
Swiss chard. See Tahini Greens, 128

tomatoes
    Avocado Caesar, 143
    Black Bean Burrito, 62
    Black Bean Soup, 144
    California Wrap, 74
    Caprese Bites, 106
    Cauliflower "Couscous," 132
    Chickpea "Omelette", 95
    Chunky Guacamole, 114
    Cucumber Cups, 121
    Ensalada Mexicana, 151
    Fiesta Layer Dip, 102
    Gazpacho Fresca, 147
    Moroccan Soup, 131
    Pasta Primavera, 58
    Red Lentil Daal, 135
    Roasted Ratatouille, 65
    Roasted Tomato Soup, 139
    Speedy Cheezy Pasta, 70
    Stuffed Red Peppers, 42
    Sun-Dried Tomato Pasta Pesto, 66
    Sunshine Salad, 152
    Sweet Potato Chili, 61
    Tex-Mex Potato Skins, 54
    Veggie Quesadillas, 83
    Zucchini Bruschetta, 125

vermicelli noodles. See Veggie Pad
    Thai, 46

yogurt. See Berry Parfait, 88

zucchini
    Fajitas Tostadas, 45
    Polenta Pizza, 53
    Roasted Ratatouille, 65
    Speedy Cheezy Pasta, 70
    Stuffed Red Peppers, 42
    Veggie Kebabs, 105
    Veggie Tempura, 122
    Zucchini Bruschetta, 125
    Zucchini Fritters, 84